I0503985

Swing Trading for Beginners

The 2019/20 Valuable Swing Trading Tips

In This Ultimate Guide, You Will Learn How to Improve Your Trading Results and Your Finances with the Best Low-Risk Application

Jim Livermore

Table of Contents

Foreword

Trading is a controversial topic for many. Some claim this to be one of the best ways to earn increased income, whereas others suspect it is nothing more than a surefire way to lose out on massive amounts of capital. Let's be clear on one thing: experienced traders *know* that trading runs the risk of losses, and therefore they do everything in their power to protect themselves against those risks. As a result, their losses are often significantly smaller and fewer than their profits, making them wildly successful in the trading business.

Educating yourself on how the market works and what to expect from the market affords you the opportunity to identify possible risks and hedge yourself against them. It also warrants you the ability to identify strong trading positions and enter them with the possibility of earning large amounts of profit from your trades.

Having a deep understanding of how the market works and developing a clear purpose in each trade is the key to creating a strong trading strategy. When it comes to trading, these are two of the most critical elements that you need to consider to ensure that you are capable of earning significant profits from your trades while also minimizing your risk of losses. *Swing Trading for Beginners* seeks to equip you with the best knowledge around how the market works, how to define your purpose in trading, and how to execute trades like a pro.

Preface

Entering the trade market feels like a game of gambling – that is until you know exactly what you are doing. Experienced marketers know that no trade is a true gamble. In fact, every single trade has been carefully researched, validated, planned out, and executed using specific strategies that help that trader maximize their profitability.

This attention to detail also supports them with minimizing their risk exposure.

Swing Trading for Beginners is an educational text that will help you identify exactly how you can carefully plan each step of your own trades so that you are able to trade like an expert from day one. By following each step of your plan, you not only trade like someone with experience, but you also ensure that every single step is clear and easy to follow.

You will discover that trading, in general, is the same from strategy to strategy, but the way each specific trade is executed will depend on that trade itself. As such, the strategy of building a structure to enter your trade with will vary from trade to trade, however, the importance and execution of this structure will remain the same across the board. By planning everything out, from the foundational knowledge upon which you are trading to the exact steps you will execute, you increase your probability of profiting and maximize your success as a trader.

Jim Livermore does an excellent job describing what this structure looks like, how you can build it, and how to execute that structure in this title. You are sure to feel confident and ready to trade by the time you are done, as he leaves no stone left unturned. This book is a must-read for anyone who is looking to enter the world of trading with a solid base of education and skills to help them become a success.

Introduction

Entering the trading world can be intimidating, overwhelming, and exciting all in one. When you step into the reality that you are going to be directly responsible for increasing your capital with each trade, and that each trade has the potential increase your capital so drastically, it is exciting.

However, many traders are not only keenly aware of the number of profits they can earn, but they are also aware of how much they stand to lose if things go wrong. As a beginner, this knowledge can be intimidating considering the fact that you may not have much if any, experience in the market. There is a lot to learn before you can really begin to cultivate a sense of confidence in your understanding of the market and in your ability to complete successful trades on the market.

With that being said, it is crucial that you remember that we all started somewhere. At one time, the idea of trading on the markets was intimidating to virtually everyone who started, at least to a degree. Over time, however, they began to develop confidence in themselves and their abilities, and now, many are earning massive profits every single month from their trades.

One of the strategies that people are using to enter trades and earn profits is swing trading. Swing trading is a form of a medium-term strategy that helps individuals earn massive profits without having to wait quite so long for those profits to become available to them. Based on how this strategy is structured, many experienced traders actually use swing trading as a method for replacing their monthly incomes and becoming completely self-sufficient as professional traders. While you do not have to become a professional to become a swing trader, it is exciting to realize just how much is possible with this particular trading strategy.

In *Swing Trading for Beginners*, you are going to learn everything that you need to know to begin swing trading. You will discover what swing trading is, how it works, and actual actionable and practical strategies to help you start swing trading like an expert from day one. By applying these strategies, you are sure to build your confidence in your abilities and develop your skills even further as you go. From there, it is up to you to decide exactly what you are going to do with all of those profits you earn.

Before you begin, I strongly advise you to read through this entire book before ever applying any of the strategies that you learn here. This book is designed to give you complete front-to-back knowledge, all of which will help you become a better trader. After you have read through it the first time, you can go ahead and start reading it a second time and actually applying the strategies as you go. This way, you are already fully aware of what needs to happen and you are far more likely to be successful.

Chapter 1: What is Swing Trading?

Swing trading is one of the three core trading strategies that people use, with the other two strategies being day trading and positional trading. This particular strategy keeps traders in their position for a few days up to a couple of weeks, as a way to capitalize on medium-term market trends. A swing trader always looks at the long-term position to validate the quality of their trade, yet only plans on staying in the position long enough to earn profits before exiting their position.

Exercising the swing trading strategy is one of the most effective ways to become a trader and use trading as a way to supplement your income or completely replace your income altogether. The benefits of this strategy are endless, making it an excellent strategy for anyone to get started with.

What Is Trading, Exactly?

Trading is a strategy that investors use to capitalize on the economy by buying and selling a form of securities with other traders. Securities, which are financial instruments, range in type but typically, they are associated with businesses either through owning shares in a business or through providing some form of loan to a business through your investments.

When you start trading, you will pick a specific type of trading that you are going to use, as well as a financial instrument that you are going to focus on for your trades. You will also choose specific strategies that fit into those two categories so that you can execute each individual trade. Each trade you conduct is going to follow a different strategy depending on what is going on in the economy, how it is affecting the market, and what positions become available for you based on that information.

Depending on what trading strategy you use, you may have access to a national, international, or even global market that will enable you to conduct your trades. Regardless of what market you are in, the same level of care, caution, and strategy must be exercised to ensure that you are making the best possible moves in your trades which will help you access the highest possible profits.

There are three different strategies of trading, each of which is used to describe the length of the position you are going to be holding in your trades. This means that these strategies describe whether you are going to be in your trades for a few hours, days, weeks, or months. Day trading is the shortest trading strategy, with all trades being done within a few hours. Positional trading is the longest strategy, with all trades lasting several weeks, months, and sometimes, even years. Swing trading is the medium-term strategy that is completed within a few days and up to about two or three weeks.

What is Swing Trading?

Swing trading is one of the three fundamental trading strategies and happens to be one of the most common trading strategies that traders use. This strategy affords people the ability to rapidly increase profits so that they can increase their income while also investing even more into future trades. Over time, the number of investable income increases to the point where traders have the capacity to profit massively off of their trades. As well, they are able to keep a significant amount of that profit in order to reach their financial goals such as replacing their income, retiring, traveling, or affording other more expensive life goals.

When you swing trade, your focus is largely based on identifying patterns in the market that indicate that a shift – or a swing – is about to happen in the direction of the market's prices. Your goal is to get in when that swing is mid-action and then exit when the swing has matured so that you can gain your profits without holding the position for too long. A successful swing trade is one where profits are earned and the market does not swing back into the opposite direction at any point during you holding your position. This way, you earn maximum profits without having to wait so long for the market to move back into a positive direction for those profits to be earned and cashed out.

The best stocks to trade as a swing trader are those that are known as large-cap stocks, which means they are some of the most active stocks that are being traded on the major stock exchange platforms. These stocks have well-defined, broad swings between high and low extremes in their price points which makes them the perfect stock for a swing trader to invest in. Swing traders will decide on their positions and strategies by identifying whether the market is bearish (in a downtrend) or bullish (in an uptrend) and will execute their trades accordingly. By doing so, they ensure that no matter what is taking place in the market they have the capacity to earn profits from their trades.

How Do You Start Swing Trading?

An individual can begin swing trading by first identifying what swing trading is and taking the time to accumulate adequate knowledge around how this strategy works. Then, they can begin actually getting involved in the stock market so that they can earn profits from the swing trading strategy.

When they are ready to take the leap, a new swing trader will need to locate the tools and platforms required to get started. These include a brokerage platform that gives the trader access to the exchange as well as tools that can be used to increase their capacity to perform technical analysis which is a method used to identify and validate trading positions.

They will also need at least $2500-$5000 in startup cash to begin trading. In the United States of America, traders must maintain a $2000 minimum in their brokerage account in order to continue trading. Starting out with more than this will ensure that you never dig into that $2000 and put yourself under the legal minimum which would force you to stop trading until you could top your funds up.

After everything is fixed in place, a trader will require a strong understanding of how to identify positions and use technical analysis to verify those positions so that they can begin a trade. From there, it will be as simple as placing the funds into the investment to open the position and managing that position until they are ready to exit it.

Swing trading sounds extremely easy to do when the definition and example of how it works have been simplified, but rest assured that there is a learning curve to this strategy. You should be prepared to undergo that learning curve so that you know what it will truly take for you to become successful at swing trading.

Buying Long, Selling Short

One crucial thing that every swing trader needs to know before they begin trading is the importance of buying long and selling short. What this means is that you want to enter positions with the intention of holding on to them for a period of time, meaning that you should conduct the right research and analysis to feel confident that your position will be a fairly low-risk position for the long haul. Ensuring that your position is a good long-term position means that if anything does not go as planned, you are still okay to be in that position for a few days or weeks until your anticipated patterns play out.

When you are selling your stocks or exiting positions, you want to have every intention to sell your stocks as fast as possible. This way, you can exit the market immediately which gives you a greater chance of securing your profits from that trade. If you take too long to sell your stocks, you may find yourself sitting in the position so long that your profits disappear and you have to take the loss to remove yourself from the position.

Trading according to the buy long, sell short strategy is critical in helping you lock in a greater sense of security around your trades while minimizing your risk and maximizing your profits. This is a cornerstone in successful swing trading and will be a necessary strategy for you to execute if you are going to earn any profit using this method.

How to Enter Trades

Entering trades as a swing trader will rely on you identifying the right patterns in the market to indicate that a swing is about to take place. There are some incredible patterns that you can look for that you are going to learn about in this very book. Those patterns let you know that a shift is about to take place, meaning that it is a great time for you to get invested in the market. Which exact pattern you are going to be looking for will depend on what stock you are looking to trade and what is happening with that stock at that particular time. It is important that you learn about all of the different patterns and grow comfortable with identifying them so that you can keep your eyes peeled for when the stocks shift. This way, when you begin to see a pattern taking place, you can identify what trading strategy works best for that pattern and prepare to trade that stock to earn yourself profits.

After you have found the right pattern to indicate where the best position is for you, you want to validate the quality of that position using technical analysis. Doing so will ensure that you are trading a stock that is going to be able to supply you with the best potential for earning profits with the lowest possible risk exposure. When you have verified that a position is going to be a strong one for you to take, you can then buy into the stocks associated with that position so that you are officially entered into an open trade. You are considered to be entered in an "open trade" until you sell your stocks and close out that position.

Investment and Margin Accounts

When you start swing trading, you are going to need to open an account with a brokerage so that you can trade. Most swing traders open accounts with online brokerages so that they can see the market and conduct trades from the convenience of their own computer or smartphone, which you are going to want to do.

Upon opening your account with a brokerage, there are two types of financial accounts linked to your brokerage that you want to know about. These two accounts include investment accounts and margin accounts.

Investment accounts are the amount of money that you personally place into your brokerage account to hold as a balance for trading. These are the funds that your trades are going to come out of so that you can begin buying and selling stocks with your account. If you do not place funds into your investment account, or if you do not maintain enough funds in your account, you will not be able to engage in trades on the brokerage's platform.

Margin accounts are another form of a brokerage account, however, the way funds are placed into the account is different. In a margin account, the broker lends the customer capital so that they can purchase stocks or other securities on the brokerage's platform. This money is a loan, so the customer needs to be prepared to pay the money back at some point in the future. However, the capital can help you get a bigger start so that you can begin making larger trades and earning larger profits much sooner. This money should be seen as a tool to leverage enabling you to earn larger profits and nothing else. You should also be prepared to pay it back as soon as possible as this will behave as a loan, meaning that you will owe interest on it so long as the loan balance remains outstanding.

Chapter 2: Why Choose Swing Trading?

Hopefully, the concept of swing trading itself is starting to feel a lot more clear to you. If not, don't worry; the entire strategy will start to make a lot more sense as you begin to read about practical applications of swing trading and what exact patterns you are looking for as well as what exact strategies you will execute trades with. In the meantime, before we dig really deep into how swing trading truly works and how you can earn profits from this strategy, let's talk about an important topic: *why swing trading?*

With three different fundamental trade strategies available for use, why should you choose swing trading over another form of trading, such as day trading or positional trading? Asking this question and discovering the answer is an important part of you conducting research to prepare yourself to become a trader. As a trader, you should always be asking as many questions as possible, because questions lead to answers and answers lead to more information and education on the topic. The more that you can educate yourself on what you are doing, why you are doing it, and how you should do it, the better of a trader you are going to become.

Even the most experienced traders in the industry are still asking questions on a continual basis so that they can grow to understand their practice even more which affords them a larger ability to scale their skills. The more skilled they become, the more they are likely to earn profits while also avoiding massive losses, which results in them becoming an even more successful trader.

All that aside, there are some very real reasons for why you should pick swing trading over any other trading strategy. These reasons will help clarify the benefits and drawbacks of this strategy, as well as how it compares against other trading strategies so that it becomes increasingly clearer as to why swing trading is one of the most popular trading strategies to date.

Benefits of Swing Trading

Some of the benefits of swing trading have already been covered here including the fact that it is a medium-term trading strategy that allows you to maximize profitability while also being able to cash out on those profits on a more frequent basis. In addition to this, swing trading hedges you against the intense volatility that is associated with shorter positions, as well as the unpredictability of longer positions. As a result, you are able to protect yourself from increased risk exposure while also improving your profitability.

Swing trading also increases the number of trades that you can enter and profit from because you are not holding positions too long. Using this strategy, you can increase your profits by frequently getting into the most promising positions, and then exiting them when they are no longer as strong. Rather than attempting to wait for the market out, you can simply move into the next strongest position and profit from that, too. As a result, you are able to profit off of the maximum profitable moments of the market and leave the rest behind.

Another benefit of swing trading that should be considered is that, due to the sheer popularity of this strategy, there is a lot of education and resources available for individuals who are swing trading. As a new swing trader, having access to large amounts of information around the strategy you are going to be executing means that any questions you might have will likely already be answered in some of those resources. This reduces the mysterious element around the strategy and makes it far more tangible and accessible, which will earn you bigger profits in the long run.

Drawbacks of Swing Trading

Anytime you trade, no matter what type of trade you are engaging in, you are at risk of losing money. Even if you are absolutely confident that everything is going to go according to plan, things can change in a heartbeat and lead to you finding yourself reigning in the losses, rather than the gains. This disadvantage is not exclusive to swing trading, but it is certainly worth mentioning and considering whenever you are planning on getting into trading. I do not say this to scare you or caution you against trading, instead, I say it because the more realistic you are about the risks involved with trading, the more likely you are to hedge yourself against them and reduce your likelihood of incurring losses.

Another disadvantage of swing trading is that you cannot guarantee that patterns are going to lead to what you expect, meaning that you might trade on a certain pattern three times and win and then the fourth time you lose. The market is not predictable, nor do patterns guarantee what is to follow, instead they simply indicate what is likely to happen. There is plenty that you can do to validate patterns and to test them to ensure your likelihood of earning profits from your trades, but there are no ways to guarantee that everything will go as planned.

A big drawback of swing trading that many people are unaware of is the intense stress that it can expose your mind to. As a swing trader, you are more likely to experience massive levels of stress due to the constant fluctuations in prices. Because you are attempting to trade on the middle-term position, it can be extremely stressful to see prices fluctuating or even starting to move in directions you did not plan for. Trying to navigate the market when you are stressed can be challenging, which is why trader psychology and mindset tools are so powerful for traders. We will discuss those in this book to help you offset the intensity of stress that you may experience and increase your ability to trade objectively, which will help increase your profitability.

Swing Trading vs. Day Trading

As you know, day trading is the shorter alternative to swing trading. When people get involved in day trading, they are trading over a few hours, whereas people involved in swing trading are trading over a few days or weeks.

Day trading tends to be a highly volatile, short-term position that can lead to massive losses if one is not careful. Unless you have the time and energy to invest in making multiple trades every day, it is challenging to become successful as a day trader. You need to be able and willing to check in on your trades several times per day to manage and exit trades all day long with this short-term strategy. If you fail to check-in or manage your positions properly, you could find yourself engaging in serious losses on a consistent basis.

While there are many risk management strategies day traders can use to minimize their exposure to the volatility of the market, it is still a highly time-consuming trading method. You need to be prepared to check in on the market every morning to identify the best trading positions and conduct technical analysis on several positions every morning so that you can enter your trades. This means that every morning, you need to be ready to identify, completely plan out, and enter several trades. This is a time-consuming task which can lead you spending hours every morning preparing for the market to open, only to have to spend hours throughout the day monitoring and managing your positions.

For those who have plenty of time to trade day, trading can certainly lead to massive profits and consistent cash-out opportunities, but only if you have the time. For those who are not interested in being involved in such a demanding and stressful investment style, swing trading is a much better alternative. With swing trading, you are still capitalizing on fairly frequent market shifts, but you are not exposed to the constant stress of opening and closing positions every single day.

Yes, you will need to check in daily, enter new positions daily, and exit positions daily. This is how you manage your positions and ensure that they are all performing and profiting properly. However, because you are not in need of both entering and exiting every single trade every single day, the pace of this trading style is a little more relaxed.

Swing Trading VS. Position Trading

Position trading is the long-term trade alternative to swing trading, and it can be a highly profitable trading style. In fact, many experienced traders purposefully enter a few positional trades in addition to their swing trades as an opportunity to increase their overall profitability.

Positional trading is known for producing incredibly high profits for those who are involved in this trading strategy. Because you are withstanding the market for so long, you are able to gain access to inflation which often results in huge profits by the time you are truly ready to exit your trade position.

With that being said, positional tradition is long-term and does require you to remain invested in a trade deal for anywhere from several weeks or months up to several years. One of the most noteworthy positional trading story themes comes from those who invested in Apple stocks back in the 1990s. People who invested in one hundred shares of Apple stocks at $78.25 in 1995 were able to cash out on those stocks for $11,244.08 in 2015. While this was a 20-year position, it earned the stockholders a profit of

$11,165.83 over those 20 years. In some cases, if you can hold onto a position for the long haul, you can earn massive profits from that position, so long as it experiences consistent growth over the years.

Still, positional trading does still require a long-term commitment, so it is not a position you want to enter into if you are going to need access to your profits sooner rather than later. If you plan on cashing out on a consistent basis so that you can travel, replace your income and work from home, or send your kids to grad school, you are going to want to favor something more consistent and predictable like swing trading. Even though swing trading will result in losses, each time you cash out, you have a guaranteed amount to apply toward whatever financial goals you are currently in the process of achieving.

Chapter 3: The Most Important Thing: Theorize Action

In the world of swing trading, there is a specific trading method known as price action trading that can help people trade on profitable stocks and earn massive profits. Price action trading is a distinctive form of swing trading, and it can provide the trader with massive amounts of profit if it is used properly. Furthermore, price action trading does nurture many excellent skills that can support you in swing trading more effectively overall, so it is worthwhile to learn about how price action trading works and who uses this trading method.

What is Price Action Trading?

Price action trading is a method where traders rely heavily on the information they receive through technical analysis regarding the way a price of certain security has behaved in the recent and distant past. This strategy completely ignores fundamental analysis, which is a form of analysis that gathers the information that is specific to an organizations' financial landscape, and instead focuses solely on technical analysis as a means for qualifying trading positions.

The way that technical analysis is completed for price action trading is relatively different from how it is done for other trade methods as well. This strategy relies less on technical indicators and more on the actual movement of the stocks themselves so that traders can develop a theory on what the prices are doing. In many ways, the decisions that price action traders make are based more on their instinctive feelings about where the market is going and less on their fact-based evidence that they accumulate from any form of research or analysis.

Although price analysis trading might sound flaky due to the fact that it is more based on theories than factual information, there is still a strong basis for how these theories are identified and validated. Generally, a trader will take a look at a stock market chart that is free of any technical indicators and will track how the price of a certain stock has behaved until that point. They will pay attention to different behaviors that indicate the trading psychology of other traders, which will then help them understand what is likely going to happen next on the market.

That's right; the tool that price action traders' rely on is their instinct around the general psychology associated with all of the traders that are actively trading on the market. They use certain psychology markers to understand whether traders are presently trading out of fear or greed, and when that psychology is likely to switch into the opposite trading pattern. By following these patterns, they can assume what traders are going to do, which will, therefore, directly affect what will happen in the market.

Once a price action trader has accumulated their information surrounding the likely psychology of the traders on the current market, they begin to locate the best positions for them to get into and trade on. They take their analysis into account and guess how long that trade will likely go on for and how long they are likely to profit so that they can determine whether or not the trade is worth the investment. When they feel absolutely confident in a trade, they will go ahead and enter the position.

What Tools Are Used for Price Action Trading?

Price action traders are not bound by any specific rules like other traders that rely on fundamental or technical analysis information to help them identify whether or not a trade position is worth the investment. For that reason, not everyone is going to arrive at the same price conclusion because each trader will have their own unique understanding of how trader psychology works and how it might impact their opinions. Due to the nature of how these trades work, they are largely subjective in nature, whereas other trade strategies are objective in nature.

Despite the trades being more subjective and based on someone's instinct and opinion rather than analysis, there are still tools that are used to determine whether a trade is going to be worth the investment or not. Traders use tools like charts, trend lines, high and low swings, price bands, and technical levels to determine the strength of a stock and where the psychology of the traders trading that stock rests. This way, they are able to validate their theories and determine whether they are likely to be true or not.

By observing the aforementioned charts, traders seek to understand how other traders are trading, what emotions they are likely feeling around trading, and how those emotions are likely going to impact their trades. While every trader's goal is to trade as objectively as possible, at the end of the day, emotions always come into play and those emotions can be seen in the overall fluctuations of the market.

When traders are greedy, the market goes bullish, and when they are fearful, the market goes bearish. How bullish or bearish the market is and how bullish or bearish it has been in the past indicates how committed traders are to their feelings of greed or fear, which helps a price action trader identify whether or not they are likely to change their mind in the near future.

Who Uses the Price Action Trading Method?

Price action trading is actually done by a wide range of people, from professionally employed traders to retail traders and even speculators. The people who are most likely to experience success with price action trading are those who have a keen eye for understanding human psychology and how our feelings can affect our decisions. Also, these traders take the time to understand psychology and emotions relating specifically to the market so that they can have a stronger understanding of what is likely going on with other traders.

If you are interested in price action trading, or even if you are not, learning about the psychology of traders is important. Doing so can help you better understand what is going on in the market and can support you with validating the quality of your trade deals. Even those who plan on using technical analysis or fundamental analysis to validate their positions can still include psychological analysis to develop a stronger sense of confidence in their trades. This way, they are more likely to capitalize and less likely to incur such massive losses with their trade deals.

Chapter 4: Market Psychology for Swing Trading

Market psychology is not only valuable for price action traders, but it is also valuable for swing traders as a whole. In fact, anyone who trades can benefit from understanding market psychology so that they can get a stronger understanding of why the market behaves the way it does and how they are most likely going to be able to capitalize from the market.

Increasing your own understanding of market psychology is a great opportunity for you to discover more about how the market works, how people trade, and what influences the volatility of the market beyond news headlines, economy, and past patterns.

In addition to helping you understand the market better and trade more effectively, understanding market psychology can also help you understand yourself better. Realize that no matter how strong of a trader you are or how effective you believe you are at managing your emotions, there is always going to be some form of influence coming from your emotions. By identifying how and why these influences occur, you can develop a method for managing these psychological patterns in yourself so that you can reduce the impact that they have on your trading style.

Self-awareness is just as important as market awareness, as you will come to understand the longer you engage in trading on the market. With that being said, here is everything you need to know about market psychology and how it affects you and other traders on the market.

Capitalizing on Being the Most Disciplined

First things first, you need to understand that the number one goal of every single trader is to become the most disciplined trader on the market. The more disciplined you can become as a trader, the more likely you are going to be able to out-smart other less disciplined traders on the market so that you can profit while they trade due to fear or greed.

If you want to become the best trader or at least a great trader, your goal needs to be to learn how to trade the market with the most discipline over anyone else. You need to learn how to constantly increase your discipline so that you are not acting on anything other than objective logical and rational reasoning about the decisions that you are making. This way, you are more likely to be able to hold stressful positions longer and earn maximum profits from those positions. You will also be more likely to leave bad trades with smaller losses, rather than stubbornly holding out for the market to "correct itself" only to find yourself even deeper in losses.

You can become the most disciplined by constantly committing to understanding what influences trade decisions, why emotions affect trade deals, and how emotions affect trade deals. Also, you can start identifying your own emotions and start managing them more effectively so that they are less likely to affect your choices and impact your decisions.

In seeking to become the most disciplined person on the market, do so in a way that takes you beyond becoming the most disciplined person only when it comes to the market itself. Seek to become more disciplined in every area of your life so that your habits of discipline spill over into your trades and make trading with discipline easier. If you attempt to be disciplined in your trades but lack discipline elsewhere in your life, you are going to find yourself constantly struggling with bringing bad habits into your trades, resulting in you exposing yourself to emotional risks and losses.

Types of Traders

The best way to understand market psychology is to understand the types of traders. At various points in the market, each type of trader will be identifiable based on the price patterns that you see in the market. These traders will take the "dominant" position for determining price direction for a period of time before another type of trader comes into action and takes that position of dominance. As such, you will see each type of trader existing in the market and affecting the overall price of the entire market.

Understanding which traders are involved in each play and what their psychology is will prove to be a powerful opportunity for you to read the market and trade regardless of whether you are price action trading or swing trading.

Breakout Traders

Breakout traders are ones who literally buy the breakouts of the market. They are the ones who are responsible for buying the market immediately before a breakout takes place and the market swings into a short reversal. The reversal can almost always be identified by elongated candlesticks on a candlestick chart which proves that the price has increased or decreased slightly *too* much in one period and it needs to come to a more true position.

How breakout traders trade also results in the breakout the market experiences, because they suddenly become afraid of having bought the stock too high and now, they are hoping someone will buy it even higher. In other words, they have entered the position and now, they are afraid that they are about to lose money, so instead, they try to immediately exit the position to attempt to hedge their losses. When all of those stocks go up for sale by fearful breakout traders, more attention is garnered by the market which results in more people coming in to purchase that specific stock.

Novice Traders

Novice traders are those who genuinely have no idea what they are doing, and it can generally be seen by how their buying and selling affects the market. Generally, novice buyers are the ones who have bought the shares from the breakout traders, and they are Ichimoku paying way too much for the stocks. These are the buyers that are responsible for the candlesticks at the top of the chart right before the reversal, and they almost always experience a loss after that point.

Note that being a new trader does not automatically lump you in with the notice trader psychology, however, you may experience a short phase early on where this happens. Generally, novice traders get into their positions because they are afraid of taking a loss so they wait too long for the market to prove itself. By the time they feel it has proved itself, it is already too late and they are buying into a market that is about to swing back into a reversal.

Momentum Traders

Momentum traders like to purchase the pullback of the chart when stocks go for a reversal before swinging back into the original direction. They are similar to swing traders, except that they are hoping for the momentum of the stock to switch directions so that they can profit.

Generally, momentum traders place their stop losses right at the base of the candlestick's bottom "wick" on a candlestick that proves that excessive overselling happened so that they can avoid losing out on profits. They bank heavily on the stock moving back in the opposite direction.

The psychology of the momentum trader is a hopeful one, in that they hope the stock will head back into a new direction. They rely on the candlestick's momentum bar being an indicator that the stock is about to reverse back into a favorable direction so that they can earn their profits. If they are wrong, their stop loss will prevent them from losing too many profits.

Swing Traders

Swing traders, like you, are the ones who are going to trade the market when there are three candlesticks on the candlestick chart where the center one falls below the bold base of the two outside ones. When you see stock do this, it indicates a reversal is about to happen because the market oversold, which means it is time for you to buy-in.

The psychology of the swing trader is that most of the novice and momentum traders have already sold their stocks and left that trading scene, so now the resistance is likely to turn into support. This means that the stock is far more likely to continue in a positive direction, with much less activity and action than it did previously. The hope of the swing trader, then, is that this is true and the stock will now consistently rise in value until they are ready to sell their shares in the next few days or weeks.

The Psychology of Greed and Fear

Regardless of what trading profile you fall under, there are two things that influence every single trader: greed, and fear. Greed is directly responsible for the rising price of stock values, whereas, fear is directly responsible for the dropping price of stock values. When you can develop an understanding around what greed and fear look like in trading and how they affect people's trading personalities, you have the capacity to set yourself up for a significant amount of success in your trades.

The Greedy Trader

In trading, greed is usually the mindset that people enter when they have an excessive desire to acquire wealth to the point that it may cloud their rationality and sense of judgment at times. With this mindset, traders have a tendency to develop an arrogant attitude that leads them to believe that their ability to earn endless profits off of their trades, or at least massive profits, is essentially guaranteed. As a result, they trade in a way that drives the prices of stock up incredibly high, to the point where it reaches an overbought state. Some of these people who are trading with a greedy mindset are known for buying high-risk trades or buying in at the last possible minute which can result in massive losses to their bottom line.

Characteristics that you tend to see from a greedy trader are often highly risky. They are known for staying in trades longer than advisable in an attempt to earn larger profits, buying into untested companies that could be high risk, and buying shares without completing any research to validate the quality of those shares. In some cases, individuals who are greedy will use high-risk trading strategies like price action trading but they will *not* complete the total psychological analysis and price analysis of the market to see if it is strong enough to trade-in. Instead, they tend to hear a bit of information regarding a certain stock, look for clues that validate what they wish to be true, and then begin trading. This confirmation bias and following the social crowd can and frequently does result in massive losses for these traders, sometimes, to the point that they can no longer trade because they have lost everything.

Greedy traders are easiest to spot at the end of a bullish market trend when they are buying into stocks that are already massively inflated in price. These traders see how much other traders have been making in these stocks and throw caution to the wind in an effort to earn some of those profits for themselves. In the end, they find themselves losing because they were greedy and they did not execute responsible trade strategies.

The Fearful Trader

The opposite of a greedy trader is a fearful trader. These are the traders who are terrified of losing out or making the wrong move, so they tend to act erratically and often out of favor with what actually needs to happen in order for them to profit. These traders are completely driven by fear and so they are constantly trading to avoid losses, rather than trading to earn profits. The very act of trading itself tends to be high stress for these traders, and they frequently quit trading because they cannot handle the intensity of what goes on in the market.

When a fearful trader trades in a particularly volatile stock, which truthfully can be any stock on the market, they are known for hyperactively watching the market. They obsess over numbers and profits, and they tend to jump out of the market at any possible sign of a switchback, which often results in them either minimizing profitability or experiencing losses because they could not wait it out.

Even if they have thoroughly researched a trend and feel confident that there will be some reversals but the market will ultimately be positive over time, a fearful trader will begin to doubt themselves as soon as they enter the market. The intensity of having actual funds invested in their trades stresses them out and makes it virtually impossible for them to successfully trade the market.

Fearful traders can be identified in the market like the ones who are acting sporadically and often rapidly. If you see the market experiencing resistance and in that period of resistance it becomes highly volatile, what you are witnessing is a tug of war between greedy and fearful traders attempting to take action on the market. Fear can truly be noticed during bearish markets, however, when trends continually drop down until they reach an oversold position because the fearful traders have been playing the dominant position in the market.

Trader's Psychology and Technical Analysis

Trading psychology continues to be one of the most important parts of technical analysis, as technical analysts rely on chart techniques to complete their trade decisions. Since the market is influenced by fearful and greedy traders, the technical analyst seeks to identify what is going and which psychology currently has control over the market's direction right now. They also want to identify how long that is likely to continue and much it will affect prices before swinging back into the reverse direction.

The psychology of traders plus the actual prices themselves help technical analysts gain as clear and thorough of an image on the market as possible so that they can trade accordingly. Without the underlying awareness around trading psychology and how it impacts the movement of the market, technical analysis will never be quite as complete or effective. For this reason, no matter what type of trader you are or what strategy you are using to capitalize on the market, you need to understand the psychology of traders and how it influences the overall market position.

Chapter 5: Save Your Money, Manage Your Emotions

You may have noticed in Chapter 4 that the psychology of a trader is largely controlled by their emotions. For example, greed and fear are two emotions that largely impact the psychology of a trader and what decisions they will ultimately make in the market. If you want to understand the psychology of trading more deeply, you need to be willing to understand the emotions of trading and how they impact your ability to make strong trades.

Understanding emotions around trading is not only valuable in deepening your awareness around trader psychology, but it will also help you deepen your awareness in yourself. Every trader is bound to experience emotions related to their trading activities, as this is a natural part of being a trader. The market is stressful and you are apt to feel fear, uncertainty, excitement, and certainty at varying points in your trades. When you have the capacity to be aware of and even anticipate these emotions, you increase your ability to manage these emotions. By managing them, you are less likely to engage in poor trade deals that will ultimately result in you losing out on profits, or even incurring complete losses overall.

Managing your emotions is something that needs to be done by every trader, regardless of how strong you think you are on an emotional front. No amount of emotional intelligence can prepare you for the level of stress and overwhelm that you are bound to feel by being engaged in the market. The only way that you can truly hedge yourself against this risk is to educate yourself on its reality, anticipate it, and exercise proper emotional management strategies as you go. For this reason, there are certain emotional management strategies that are advised to be used by traders, in particular, to ensure that you are not letting your emotions guide you.

How Social Influence and Numbers Cause Failure

One of the biggest things that traders do, especially new traders, that leads to failure is relying on social influence and numbers. News headlines and specific numbers are two major factors in the analysis, so it makes sense as to why people tend to get caught up in these two areas of trading to the point where it affects their emotions and, therefore, the quality of their trades. This is because very few new traders realize that these two elements are meant to be used to create a bigger picture about what is likely to be happening, not as independent reasons as to why you should or shouldn't trade a certain stock.

Your entire goal with technical analysis and fundamental analysis is to validate the quality of trades and support yourself in completing a total case for a certain stock. This case should, ideally, fight *for* the reason why the stock is worth investing in so that you can earn money from your trades.

If you find, at any point, that the case is obviously fighting against the trade, then naturally, this is not a case you should pursue or a trade you should engage in. However, the bigger picture always needs to be addressed when you make your final decision with a trade, and when you create the plan for how you are going to trade that particular stock. This way, you are most likely to have all of the right predictions in place to improve the quality of your trade and keep you successful moving forward.

My recommendation for new traders is to learn how to keep everything focused on the bigger picture, while also taking each part of the evidence seriously. Some pieces of evidence are going to completely destroy the rest of the case, no matter how great the case may seem.

For example, if you are looking at the price history for a certain stock and you are looking at the indicators around that stock and everything is looking positive but a new piece of information proves the company is heading for bankruptcy, guess what? It is probably not a good stock for you to invest in no matter how good it might seem right in this very moment. Attempting to invest in a stock like this would align with greedy trading and could result in you taking a huge risk and losing.

Additionally, if you rely too heavily on what other people are saying, you might find yourself engaging in what is known as confirmation bias. Confirmation bias ultimately means that because you heard something from someone you trust or respect, you are now going to look specifically for evidence that supports that opinion. You are unlikely to be objective in your trades, and therefore, you are more likely to experience losses. While you do want your information to come from high quality, knowledgeable, and reputable sources, you do not want to rely solely on any one thing for your final decision. Instead, you want to validate and verify everything and ensure that you are looking as objectively as possible. This way, you do not act out of greed or fear in your trade deals.

Anticipate the Emotions

Being able to anticipate what emotions you are likely to experience, when, and why is one of the best ways that you can manage your emotions as a trader. When you can anticipate how you are likely to feel and what will be causing these feelings, then you can make decisions going forward that are still likely to be rooted in logic and reasoning rather than emotions.

Many traders even develop their own personal rules around how they will handle each emotion during trades so that they are confident their emotions will not influence their decisions. We will talk more about how you can do that in a moment.

The three sets of emotions you are likely to experience as a trader include fear or nervousness, conviction or excitement, and greed or overconfidence. Every trader experiences each of these emotions frequently throughout their trading career, so there is truly no way to get around them, instead, you just have to work with them.

Fear and nervousness are most likely to be caused when you are trading in trades that are way too big, or if you are in the "wrong" trade, which means you are trading in a particular position that does not fit the plan you have made. New beginners are also likely to experience nervousness due to not entirely knowing what to expect when it comes to trading.

Conviction and excitement are two emotions you want to use to help you gauge the quality of your trades, as you want to experience each of these every time you enter a new trade. These are the final pieces of any good trade as they prove that you have entered into a position you are confident in, which means you are likely going to execute that trade perfectly. This does not guarantee your results, but it is far more promising than fear or greed.

Greed and overconfidence are emotions you experience if you find yourself exclusively trading on deals that you think will be big winners. Frequently, traders will move into a place of greed or overconfidence when they find themselves on a winning streak and want to win even more. They can even be the result of you doing well. However, if you are not careful, greed or overconfidence can lead to you making a sloppy mistake and losing out big time, possibly even ending your trading career. Be cautious around these emotions.

Develop Your Own Personal Trading Rules

Creating your own personal trading rules is a great opportunity to manage your emotions while also increasing your likelihood of entering positive trades. With your own rules, you can identify risks that you personally expose yourself to through certain emotions or habits you have, and you can create rules for how you are going to minimize your exposure.

One big rule that traders often have for themselves include setting specific risk and reward tolerance levels that they are willing to endure when they are entering and exiting trades. Having your own personal risk tolerance level ensures that you never trade beyond what is comfortable for you. This means that you are never trading too big or too risky for you to reasonably manage based on your emotional tendencies and psychological profile as a trader.

Another rule you can set for yourself would include the emotions you are likely to experience as a trader. If you are entering, managing, or exiting a trade and you feel any emotion other than conviction or excitement, you need to check your emotions first to ensure that you are not trading emotionally. You will need to create your own emotional management strategies for yourself based on what you feel is going to be reasonable for your own emotions.

This could include thoroughly validating the quality of your trade so that you can feel confident that you are trading based on logic and evidence and not based on emotions. It could also include preventing yourself from obsessively checking on trades to make sure that they are performing as you wish.

Only you will know what your emotional tendencies are, so you will have to create plans and manage your emotional tendencies accordingly to ensure that you are always trading from a strong position.

Choose to Trade the Right Market Conditions

Another way that you can improve your emotional management as a trader is by trading in the right market conditions. A mistake people make that can completely destroy the quality of their trades is through trading in the wrong market conditions, which can both be the result of emotional trading and the cause of emotional trading. When you trade in the wrong market conditions, you are inevitably going to expose yourself to much more risk because you are going to be trading on a market that isn't ideal.

You can also manage your emotions with this tip by avoiding trading when you are feeling off or not in your best state of mind. If you generally feel like you are in a more volatile state of emotions yourself, trading may not be ideal as you might find yourself being more likely to start trading in a way that favors emotions over objective reasoning. Always choose to favor the side of caution over the side of excessive or unnecessary risk to ensure that you are not setting yourself up for failure.

Trade Manageable Trade Sizes

Some people who get into trades get into ones that are far too large for them to reasonably manage, which can lead to massive amounts of fear and uncertainty. The people who are most likely to get into these positions are those who are trading out of greed or those who are completely new to the market and do not know what constitutes as a reasonable trade size.

With that being said, trading beyond your comfort level or trading beyond what is reasonable by engaging in trade sizes that are much too large can trigger massive amounts of fear in the trader themselves. Even if the trade were to go smoothly, the fear you experience alone could be enough for you to make a huge mistake, mismanage the trade, and experience a loss from it instead.

It is crucial that you only enter trade sizes that truly feel comfortable to you so that you are not exposing yourself to this particular risk. The best way to pick trade sizes is to choose ones that are reasonable for your budget and to choose ones that are reasonable to your skill level. Ideally, the more skilled you are and the larger your budget is, the larger trades you can enter. Still, there should be a cap on how high you are willing to go in a trade size to ensure that you never bite off more than you can chew.

Stay Humble and Respect the Market

This is a crucial trading rule to consider when it comes to your emotions regardless of whether you are experiencing greed or fear in your trading style. Those who are trading out of greed are likely to get overzealous or arrogant with their trades while also cultivating a sense of invincibility. Those who are trading out of fear are likely to find themselves doubting their skills and abilities and fearing the market far more than is reasonable. In either scenario, your emotions are going to negatively impact your ability to made strong trade deals and earn better profits.

As a trader, you need to always stay humble and respect the market. You should be neither too eager nor too fearful about what you are doing and the trades you are entering. You need to be modest, humble, and aware of the fact that the market is volatile and that no amount of preparing or analyzing can save you from a possible failed trade. By keeping this healthy awareness around the market and not letting it consume you, you ensure that you remain at a neutral state of respect with the market. This way, you are less likely to expose yourself to risk from your emotions.

Avoid Obsessive Behaviors that Increase Fear

Some behaviors people engage in are known for increasing feelings of fear in traders. These behaviors are often obsessive in nature and are most common in new traders who find themselves doubting their skills or abilities or in experienced traders who have recently experienced a significant loss. The biggest obsessive behavior that fearful traders engage in is obsessively over checking their news apps and stock apps to make sure that their trade is still performing as planned. The idea is to be able to spot trouble before it becomes bad and exit the market, but the reality is that all this does is increase your fear and make you jumpier in your trade position. This is not a good position to be in when you are trading stocks.

Traders who have a strong emotional management system in place periodically check in on their trades at certain pre-determined times on a day to day basis. Then, they completely leave everything alone. This way, they are not likely to find themselves accumulating massive amounts of unnecessary stress around the trades they are actively managing. Rather than filling their minds with the constant stress of the volatile market every few minutes, they are giving themselves time to prepare for the check-in, and they are giving themselves time to digest the information and remain calm and level-headed. As a result, they are far more calm and tactful in their trades. Avoid obsessive behaviors and choose calculated, logic-based ones instead to ensure that you are always keeping your emotions in check.

Manage Your Stress Outside of Trading

The final way that you can really boost your emotional management to support positive trading is by managing your stress outside of trading. Regardless of how skilled you think you are at compartmentalizing, everyone brings some level of stress with them into other activities when they have accumulated stress in any one area of their lives. By creating a strong stress management plan for your entire life, you can feel confident that you will not be allowing stress from other areas of your life to leak into your trading behaviors.

Some of the ways you can manage stress outside of trading include taking better care of yourself and having an active stress management protocol in place. Taking better care of yourself by sleeping better hours, eating a healthy diet, getting adequate exercise, and giving yourself time to genuinely feel good by taking frequent breaks and having fun is a great way to manage stress.

Through these strategies, you can feel confident that you are not inadvertently exposing yourself to stress to your body, mind, or emotions due to the way that you take care of yourself. Having a proper stress protocol in place can also help you manage stress when it does arise.

Stress protocol can be anything from taking an extra break to engage in some form of relaxing activity to talking to a close friend or even a therapist about what you are going through, depending on how stressful it is and what the context of the situation is.

In addition to helping you feel better in general, managing your stress and emotions outside of trading will help you cultivate healthy stress management practices. This way, when you begin trading as soon as you start experiencing stress, you will be able to apply your existing skills and habits to the situation to minimize your stress. As a result, you will be able to manage the stress you experience far more effectively because you will already be an expert at doing it.

Chapter 6: Swing Trading Tips: What are the Best Trading Indicators for You?

A big part of swing trading responsibly is knowing how to conduct proper technical analysis. Technical analysis involves many factors, but one of the most important factors is the use of technical indicators or trading indicators that will help you identify what is going on in the stock market. Using these indicators will help you understand previous trends, patterns, and current market conditions so that you can fully understand where the best trading positions are for you.

There are literally hundreds of trading indicators out there, but not every indicator is going to give you the best information as a swing trader. For that reason, you want to make sure that you are cutting out all of the fluff and just getting down to the indicators that are going to give you the best possible information to prepare for your trade.

When you begin using technical indicators, it is crucial that you only use one technical indicator at a time. Each indicator behaves differently and if you begin using too many, you could find yourself experiencing information overload. Furthermore, you might find that the information slightly differs from indicator to indicator which can leave you feeling confused and overwhelmed.

The best way to swing trade is to pick one technical indicator, read it, and formulate a piece of your case from that information. Then, you can go one to reinforce that information with another 2-3 indicators to validate your findings from the original indicator. This way, you are not overwhelming yourself and you are successfully building a strong case for the trading positions that you are planning on entering into.

The Best Swing Trading Indicators

There are eight technical indicators that are the best for swing trading. These indicators are going to help you read the market so that you can identify exactly where the best swing trading options exist, enabling you to maximize your profits as a swing trader. The eight indicators include Ichimoku Kinko Hyo, Bollinger band, parabolic stop and reverse (SAR), relative strength index (RSI), moving average convergence divergence (MACD), average directional index, stochastic, and on-balance volume (OBV.)

Ichimoku Kinko Hyo (Ichimoku Cloud)

Ichimoku Kinko Hyo, generally just called Ichimoku for short, is a technical indicator that allows traders to gauge momentum in the market. It also supports them in finding areas of support and resistance that are likely to exist in the future of the market so that they can identify future positions. This technical indicator has five lines included which are called the kijun-sen, tenkan-sen, chikou span, senkou span A, and senkou span B lines.

The purpose of the Ichimoku is to give people the opportunity to learn a significant amount of information about the market from just one indicator. The name literally translates to "one look" so that traders can collect a great deal of information without having to activate and deactivate various different indicators to see what is going on in the market. As a trader, the Ichimoku is a great indicator to start with to give you a strong read on a stock and to determine whether or not it is worth pursuing. If it is, you can validate your findings using other indicators.

In order to properly read this indicator, you need to know what the five lines represent and how to read them.

Kijun-sen

The kijun-sen line is the baseline and this indicator calculates its position by taking the highest high and lowest low of the last 26 periods, adding them together and then dividing the answer by 2. This creates a line that indicates what the support and resistance level of the market is, which will help identify any changes in trends. Traders will often use this line to identify where a stop loss should be placed in their trade deal.

Tenkan-sen

Tenkan-sen is the conversion line, which is calculated by taking the highest high and highest low from the last nine periods, then adding them together and dividing the answer by 2. As a result, they can identify key support and resistance levels, just as they did with the kijun-sen line. These two lines operate together to verify the information being shared in the other line, providing a more rounded view into what is happening.

Chikou Span

The chikou span is the lagging span line, which lets you know the current period's closing price all the way back 26 days on the chart. This shows the trader where areas of possible support and resistance exist so that they can plot where the next areas of opportunity are likely to exist on the chart.

Senkou Span A

The senkou span A is a line that is calculated by taking the tenkan-sen and the kijun-sen and adding the two numbers together and then dividing the answer by 2. The result is then plotted on the chart 26 days ahead to indicate the likely average direction of the chart over the next 26 days. The edge formed by this line is known as the cloud, and it helps identify future positions of opportunity with that stock.

Senkou Span B

The senkou span B takes the highest high and lowest low of the stock over the past 52 periods and adds them together, then divides the answer by 2. Then, it plots the answer 26 days into the future to provide an additional piece of information regarding the likely direction of the stock going forward. The result is a range between the senkou span A and senkou span B lines that let traders know where the price is likely to fall over the next 26 days. This way, they can make an informed decision based off of the likely high and likely low of the trading behaviors of that particular stock.

Bollinger Band

The Bollinger band is a technical analysis tool that takes two standard deviations that move away from a simple moving average line. The result is a positive line and a negative line that travel on either side of the moving average line, providing a range of where the market has been trading in the past. The Bollinger band was designed by John Bollinger, a famous technical trader, who chose to name the trademarked indicators after himself.

The Bollinger band is generally read over a 20-day simple moving average so that you can see how a particular stock has behaved over the recent past. This gives you an idea as to the moving averages between the highest and lowest points of the market, which provides you with the opportunity to fully understand what the market is doing and where it is going.

There are two periods in the Bollinger bands that you want to pay close attention to that will inform you as to whether or not the market is currently behaving in the way that you think it is behaving. This includes the squeeze and the breakouts.

The squeeze takes place when the bands come close together around the moving average "squeezing" inward. When this happens, it means that there is likely going to be increased volatility in the future of the stock, which means that there are more opportunities for swing traders to profit from that particular stock. Seeing the squeeze happen is a good sign for swing traders that there are opportunities arising in the market.

Breakouts are behavior that takes place when the trades move toward the outside of the bands. When you see this happen, it is actually not a trading signal at all, even though many people mistakenly believe it is because it is a behavior that appears to be abnormal for the band itself. You will not be able to identify any future movement due to breakouts, so do not worry about these or use them to identify future trading possibilities as the information you accumulate is likely to be unreliable.

Parabolic Stop and Reverse (SAR)

The parabolic SAR indicator is a form of indicator that is used to determine what direction the current market trend is facing and any potential reversals that may arise in that direction. This indicator shows up on your trading screen in the form of several dots that follow market trends to let you know what is currently going on in the market. The dots follow a trailing stop and reverse method that traders call SAR which identifies where the best exit and entry points in the market are.

To read the parabolic SAR, you want to open your market chart and activate the indicator. Then, you want to locate the dots that are the indicator itself that displays over your market chart around the price fluctuations. When you see dots below the price, this means that the price is moving up in value, and when you see a dot above the price, it means that the price is moving down. The dots will not count each specific move in the market but rather than movement as a whole, so sometimes, you may see some volatility falling under the indicator that is not tracked by the dots. When you see this happening, you can assume that the volatility is unlikely to result in a complete reversal, unless the parabolic SAR switches location and direction.

Relative Strength Index (RSI)

Relative strength index, also known as RSI, is a form of technical indicator that tracks the momentum of the market to measure the magnitude of all recent price changes. The purpose of the RSI is to evaluate the magnitude of overbought and oversold conditions in the price of stocks or assets so that traders can develop an understanding of the psychology behind the traders that are actively trading.

If the price momentum drops into an intensely bearish market, this suggests that the traders are presently fear-based, whereas if the price momentum rises into an intensely bullish market, this suggests that the traders are presently greedy. When the movements are more gradual or neutral, this suggests that the market is currently being traded smartly, but you can likely expect for some volatility to take place at any point in the future.

The RSI is presented as an oscillator that features a single line to track the momentum of the market. This oscillator is located below the actual market chart as a separate chart that follows the market's movement in real-time. When you look at the indicator, you will see that there are two frames on the oscillator: one at the bottom of the indicator and one at the top. The one at the bottom represents the 0-30% range of the chart, which is the oversold section.

The one at the top of the market represents the 70-100% range of the chart, which is the overbought section. Anytime the line that is the RSI moves into either position, you can assume that it is going to reverse fairly quickly. Typically, the deeper the line moves into the overbought or oversold position, the more drastically the market will switch back into the opposite direction. As a swing trader, you want to look for lines that are deep into the overbought or oversold position so that you can time your entry and exit accordingly.

Moving Average Convergence Divergence (MACD)

The moving average convergence divergence indicator, or the MACD, looks very similar to the RSI in that it exists on an oscillator type chart below the market chart with two frames representing the overbought and oversold positions on the market. Unlike the RSI, however, the MACD is considered oversold when it drops below 20 or overbought when it rises over 80.

As well, the MACD has 2 lines that reflect how the market is behaving and the way these two lines are positioned both on the market and in relation to each other will give you valuable information about what is going on with the current trading trends. One line is blue, and this line represents the moving average of the 12-period EMA. The other line is red and it represents the moving average of the trends over the 26-period EMA.

The general direction of the lines will tell you what direction the market is currently moving in, and just as with the RSI, when it rises over 80 or below 20, you can assume that it is likely going to take on a reversal fairly quickly. In addition to this basic information, the MACD can also tell you about the momentum of the market trends. When the two lines are further apart, this suggests that the distance between the EMAs is growing and that it is likely due for a correction fairly soon.

This is generally proven to be true when the two lines inevitably come back together and cross. These crosses can also tell you important information about what is going on in the market. When the blue line crosses below the red line, this means that the market is moving into a negative period, and when the red line crosses below the blue line, this means the market is moving into a positive value. You can use these crosses and the gaps between the lines to help indicate when shifts are going to happen. Naturally, these shifts are where you want to enter and exit the market to maximize your profits.

Average Directional Index (ADX)

The average directional index, also known as the ADX, is an indicator that is used to determine the strength of a trend, which, in turn, helps the trader understand how much longer that trend is likely going to last. This is important as it helps prevent people from getting in on trends too late, likely costing them big time in the end. The trends in the market can either be up or down, the ADX will help identify them both.

Like with the RSI and MACD, the ADX shows up on a separate chart below the active market chart, but it follows the active market in real-time. The ADX will look very similar to the shape of the market's candlesticks, except that it will follow a smoother trend than the candlesticks do and it will often switch just before the market itself switches.

The ADX is read using two additional indicators: the Negative Directional Indicator (-DI) and the Positive Directional Indicator (+DI). As such, there are generally three separate lines on the indicator that help traders decide what the trend is and where the best points of entry are, as well as whether they should be trading in a long or short position. As a swing trader, you want to be buying into long positions and selling in short positions. If you do not see the indicator turning in favor of these trends, you should not be trading the market.

To read the ADX, look for the ADX line's direction. If it has a +DI, this means the price of the stock or asset you are trading is increasing, whereas, if it has a −DI, this means the price of the stock or asset you are trading is decreasing. When you see crosses between the +DI and the -DI, this signals that there could be a switch in position to decide whether the bullish traders or the bearish traders currently have the upper hand.

Stochastic

The stochastic oscillator is another momentum indicator that traders use to identify the direction of the market and the magnitude of that direction. Once again, this is another indicator that appears below the market chart and follows the live market's action. The stochastic indicator has two frames on either side of the chart representing overbought and oversold positions, and a center area of the indicator that represents baseline action.

The purpose of the stochastic indicator is to compare the closing price of a security to a range of its overall prices during a certain period of time. You can adjust what period of time you want to look into in order to see how the stock or asset has behaved over any period in the past. The shorter the period, the more sensitive the oscillator will be to the directional price changes in the market. With that being said, the indicator will be more sensitive to the momentum than the actual price itself, so it generally moves far more dramatically in either direction than the market itself does.

When a stochastic indicator reaches the lower frame on the screen, this means that the current trend has likely reached peak momentum in a bearish and that it is more than likely going to pause and then head back into the bullish position. Likewise, when the stochastic indicator reaches the higher frame on the screen, this means the current trend has likely reached peak momentum in a bullish position and that it is more than likely going to pause and head back into the bearish position.

OBV: On-Balance Volume

On-balance volume (OBV) is also a momentum indicator that follows volume flow in order to predict any changes in the stock price. This indicator was designed by Joseph Granville and is based on his belief that volume is the key force behind activity in the markets and that certain flows and fluctuations in volume can indicate whether or not the current trends will continue. The OBV indicator is another indicator that shows up on a chart below the active market chart and follows the active market chart's real-time prices. On this particular chart, you will see fractions on the right side of the screen that indicate the total volume of the stocks being traded.

When the simple line in the indicator's chart moves up, it indicates that higher volumes are being bought and lower volumes are being sold, and when it reaches exceptionally high volumes toward the top of the chart, it indicates that the prices are due for a reversal. Alternatively, when it reaches the bottom of the chart, it indicates that lower volumes are being bought and higher volumes are being sold, and when it reaches exceptionally low, this means that the stock is also likely due for a reversal.

Chapter 7: Reduce Your Risks and Improve Your Skills

As a trader, reducing your risks and improving your skills should always be at the forefront of your mind. The more that you can focus on decreasing your risk on each trade and increasing your ability to trade with greater skill, the more likely you are to earn better profits from each trade. In a sense, increasing your skill is directly decreasing your risk as well because this enables you to be aware of what possible risks exist and how you can hedge yourself against them. The more consistent you are in educating yourself and practicing risk management, the more likely you will be to earn greater profits than you earn losses.

In trading, there are some key ways that you can minimize your risk while also improving your skills. Some of these include learning how to assess the risk and the reward of each trade, learning how to set stop losses and profit targets, managing trade sizes, and maintaining a trading journal for an organization. Understanding how to use each of these skills is going to help you become a better trader.

Each of these skills should be applied from day one, and you will likely learn about more skills as you go.

Assessing the Risk and the Reward

Learning how to assess the risk and reward of each trade is a crucial skill that you need to have. Every trader is going to have their own unique understanding of the risk and reward of each trade based on their personal risk tolerance and their understanding of what they are reading. With that being said, all traders typically follow the same strategies in identifying what the risks and rewards are likely to be for each trade. You can use these same strategies to identify the risks and rewards based on your own understanding and compare them to your own risk tolerance profile.

The first place to start when it comes to assessing risk and reward is with risk. If a trade is going to be too risky, it is not smart to trade it no matter how good the reward might be. Assessing risk can be done by first looking at the stock's history to see how it has behaved in the past. If a stock is too volatile, this may indicate that the stock is riskier than you are willing to trade in and that you are better to go to a different stock that is going to be more consistent. While a volatile stock is necessary for swing trading to occur, trading in *too* volatile of stock can become intimidating and can invoke your fear response, possibly causing you to mess up the trade. In this circumstance, you need to make sure that you are trading in volatile stocks that still feel manageable for you and your trading profile.

In addition to looking at the current trading profile of that stock, be sure to look at the stock's histogram chart. Pay attention to the 1 month, 3 months, 6 months, and 12-month marks on the chart to see how the stock has traded in the past. If the stock generally has a lot of volatility but continues to steadily rise over time, chances are this stock is not going to be as risky as one that barely rises or does not rise at all over time.

Another great way to measure risk is to measure the standard deviation of a stock, which is a strategy that measures the dispersion of data from its expected value. In other words, this measures where the stock *should* be if it were true to price, versus where it was actually priced. The standard deviation chart will tell you if it was oversold, on par, or overbought for where it was currently at in the market, effectively helping you measure the historical volatility of that particular chart. It will also tell you where the stock currently exists in the market so that you can see where it currently rests in terms of volatility.

Measuring the reward of a stock is typically done by following the same strategies that you did to measure the risk of the stock, except that you are looking for the likely reward value of that particular stock. In this case, you want to identify how high that stock is likely to rise to before you need to exit your trade so that you can A) plan and time your exit and B) anticipate your likely reward from that trade. Reward, like risk, is not guaranteed, but it does help you calculate how much you are likely to gain back from an investment. If that reward is significant enough, it is worth trading in. If it is too small, it may be better to wait until a better offer. Likewise, if it is too high, you should be cautious, as this indicates that something unpredictable and unlikely is going on in the stocks. Anytime a reward measures higher than the risk, you should always consider that stock to be in a high state of volatility. As we say in the trading business; if it looks too good to be true, it is.

Setting Stop Losses and Profit Targets

Stop losses and profit targets are two risk management tools that will help you automate your trading process while also protecting your investments. Each of these risk management tools can be set up on your trades to create parameters around your trades themselves. Stop losses prevent you from losing too much on stocks, whereas profit targets ensure that if your stock reaches your desired profit point it trades rather than dropping again should the market switch directions.

Both of these should be set up on every single trade you make to ensure that you are never overexposing yourself in a trade. Trading without these in place can leave you highly exposed, meaning that you are far more likely to lose out on profits or even incur risks than you are if you trade with these in place.

Your stop losses should be set based on your calculations from your technical analysis, as well as based on your risk tolerance and desired reward ratios. Setting these two risk management tools properly is key to making sure that you get the most out of every single trade without putting yourself directly at risk.

Your stop losses should always be put slightly below where you bought into the market so that you are able to withstand some volatility in the market itself. Many swing traders will place their stop losses at the bottom of the bottom candle "wick" on the candlestick chart when they enter a trade. This way, they have plenty of room to handle volatility without putting themselves at risk of major losses.

So, as soon as the swing trader sees the candlestick chart dig deep into an overbought or oversold position of volatility, they will buy into a trade and immediately place a stop loss in that lowered position. This way, they are immediately protected from any further drops in the market. Should the market drop to this point or head lower, their brokerage will automatically sell their stocks to exit them from the trade, resulting in them taking on a loss. With that being said, the loss is much less than it would likely be had they stayed in too long.

Profit targets are where many new traders tend to get greedy, but experienced traders know better. Getting greedy with profit targets can actually minimize your profitability by resulting in you missing out on respectable gains in your investments and instead of experiencing significant losses. For example, let's say that you set a profit target higher than you think a stock will reach and then the stock reaches up but never reaches your target. Then, it reached back downward and you miss out on profits or even drop right to your stop loss because your profit target was misplaced. Not having a profit target responsibly placed can result in you missing out on profits, so it is not advisable to try to set it higher in order to achieve greater profits *just in case.*

With profit targets, you can set reasonable profit targets that will earn you a respectable income and have your brokerage automatically sell your stocks when you reach your profit target. This way, if the market moves around a lot in between you checking in to manage on your trades, you can feel confident that your profit target will still be exercised as long as that point is reached. Your profit target should always be set at the point where you reasonably believe the market will reach in a certain period of time based on how it has behaved in the past, where it currently rests, and what activity is currently going on with that trade. This will improve your chances at having your profit targets reached, therefore, improving your profitability in your trades.

Managing the Trade Size

Trading too large of trades at any given time does not just expose you to emotionally-based risks, but it also exposes you to the possibility of experiencing a massive loss. If each of your trades begins to spend too much of your capital, you will find that you are over-invested in certain areas of the market, and therefore, you are at greater exposure.

Let me break this down for you in a simple way.

If you were to take $5,000 and invest $1000 each into 5 different trades, you would need all five trades to perform well in order to earn profits. If 2-3 of those experienced any losses, never mind significant losses, you would likely end up with less than you started with, which is never the goal with trading. If instead, you were to invest $200 each into 15 lower-risk trades and save the additional $2000 as a float, you would be more likely to earn profits back. Also, the value of each loss would be significantly lower which would mean that you would still have plenty of capital to bounce back from those losses with. As a result, you would likely end up profitable right from the start and those profits would increase over time, meaning that you would always stay in the green.

Maintaining a Trading Journal

Maintaining a trading journal is frequently looked at as an educational resource, but it also operates as a risk management resource when used properly. As a result, it can help you manage your risks and increase your skills, making it the perfect tool to leverage when you are trading.

The purpose of a trading journal is ultimately to track your every single move in the market. You also want to maintain watchlists and track possible moves in the market, while also cultivating trading plans around those possible moves if they seem like they could be a good fit for you in the immediate to near future. It is important that you track everything you do, everything you learn, and every theory or hunch that you develop when you are trading in your trading journal. For that reason, I actually keep four journals so that I can keep everything organized and manageable.

From a risk perspective, your trade journals will help you recall exactly what your trading plan and strategy for every single trade was. This way, you do not forget what you are doing mid-trade and find yourself making poor moves due to not having positioned yourself in the best possible location in the market. It also helps you look upon historical trades to see how they performed so that you can avoid making the same mistakes in the future, effectively helping you increase your likelihood of succeeding in each trade going forward.

From an educational perspective, your trade journal will help you grow from where you are by letting you keep track of everything you learn both through experience and research along the way. It will also help you keep track of possible trade deals and track practice trades, which are trades you plan out and pretend to enter, manage, and exit, without ever actually doing so. This way, you can build your skill before ever actually getting into the market with capital to invest, making you both more knowledgeable and more confident when it comes time to actually trade.

Chapter 8: Technical Analysis: Charting Basics

You may have noticed throughout this book that one of the primary components of trading is using charts to follow the market trends and pinpoint your next best positions. Charts are used to convey what is currently happening in the market pricing. Unlike indicators, these actually present the real-time prices of the stock markets themselves.

There are a few different types of charts that you can follow to follow the stock market and get a real-time feel for what is going on with the stocks at any given time. The two most popular types, however, are candlestick charts and bar charts. These two charts are the most commonly used charts, and many technical indicators that presently exist are made with these charts in mind. With that being said, they can be used on other charts but they will be easier to read and gather as much information from as possible if you use these charts to help you read the indicators better.

To help you really become an experienced trader, we are going to discuss what these charts are, how they work, and what patterns you are likely to see in these charts.

Types of Charts

In total, there are four types of charts that are used to represent the prices of the stock market. Candlestick charts and bar charts are the types we use when actively trading, but there are also line charts and point and figure charts. Each of these types of charts has its own unique purpose and value that they add to the market.

Line charts are typically used to represent a longer-term period in the market. They are frequently used to give evidence of how well the market is performing in presentations for many different matters relating to prices and finances. Everyone from professional traders to investors who are tracking the quality of a company will use line charts to create formal presentations representing long term trends in the stocks. Professional financial advisors will also generally use these types of charts to show the trends of the market overall to encourage new investors to feel confident that the market is generally positive and that their investments are likely to earn strong returns.

Point and figure charts were actually designed as a system for recording prices but have since evolved to become an actual charting method. This is a far more complex charting method that the average trader does not need to take into consideration too greatly, as they are not relevant to most trading styles.

Candlestick Charts

Candlestick charts were actually invented by Japanese rice merchants in the 1700s and have become a widely popular charting method for traders to follow ever since. The merchants who developed the candlestick charts wanted to be able to track the price action of rice and realized that many traders traded based on emotions and not logic or reasoning. They felt that by creating a chart that accurately tracked the market while also reflecting the emotions of traders, they could influence the market to move more in their favor, increasing the profitability of the rice business.

Candlestick charts are presented on a periodic graph and the candlesticks themselves are represented by small candle-shaped bars that are displayed across the chart to reflect price patterns. The candlesticks themselves, or the candle-shaped bars, are comprised of three separate parts, each of which gives traders a specific piece of information about the current price of the stocks. The center of the candlestick, or the "stick" itself, is known as the body. The "wick" that extends from the top of the candlestick is known as the upper tail, and the one that extends from the bottom of the body is known as the lower tail.

The body represents the opening price and closing price at the time interval or time period being represented by the bar. If the candlestick is red, this means that the top edge of the body represents the opening price and the bottom edge of the body represents the closing price. If the candlestick is green, this means that the bottom edge of the body represents the opening price and the top edge of the body represents the closing price. With that being said, red candlesticks represent a bearish market, whereas green candlesticks represent a bullish market.

The tails represent the highest and lowest prices that were bought and sold at in that period. For a green bullish candlestick, the bottom of the lower tail represents the lowest price stocks were bought at, whereas the top of the upper tail represents the highest price stocks were sold at. For a red bearish candlestick, the top of the upper tail represents the highest price stocks were bought at and the bottom of the lower tail represents the lowest price stocks were sold at.

This is why many swing traders set their stop losses at the bottom of the lower tail on a bearish candlestick in the middle of a swing; it represents the lowest stock price for that period which means that this is the lowest they can withstand. Any lower means the price of the market is dropping too far, yet there is a chance that it could still play in that lower price area before fully reversing into the positive direction.

Candlestick Patterns

Candlestick patterns reflect patterns that are occurring in the market in terms of trading prices and momentum. Every single price movement in the market is reflected in candlesticks, and the patterns you see reflect how that price movement is coming along. Virtually, every stock will have its own unique pattern that it tends to follow that can help indicate what that stock is doing now and what it is likely to do next.

While past experiences do not guarantee future results in trading, they can give you a general idea as to what is going on. In addition to reading patterns on specific stocks, traders also look for certain pattern themes that occur in virtually every stock on the market at one point or another. These patterns indicate price fluctuations in stock and can help pinpoint desirable places to enter and exit trades in any given stock. You will learn more about the specific patterns to look for in Chapter 9.

Basic Bearish and Bullish Candlesticks

In every stock, you are going to see basic bearish and bullish candlestick patterns that play out to show you what is happening in the market. The easiest way to see what is going on, however, is to track a few candlesticks over specific periods. For example, you might look at the chart as a whole, then look at the last 10-15 periods, then look at the last 3-5 periods to get an idea of what is going on with any given stock.

Remember, candlesticks that are green are bullish and candlesticks that are red are bearish. When you see these candles displayed on a chart for any given stock, you will easily begin to determine where the bullish and bearish patterns lie for that particular stock. This way, you can trade the stock accordingly. Again, you are going to be looking for very specific patterns as a swing trader, which we are going to dig further into so that you know exactly what to look for.

Reversal Candles

Reversal candles refer to the candles that happen directly at the point where the reversal in the market starts taking place. These candlesticks are different from retracement candles, which are those that only create small reversal shifts in the market before going back into the original direction. Reversal candlesticks are generally much larger, indicating that far more change took place in prices and that the momentum has increased exponentially in a short period of time. You can identify these as being a series of 2-3+ candlesticks that are all moving in the opposite direction, typically with a fair amount of momentum to them. When this takes place, it means that there is so much momentum in the reversal that it is more than likely going to stick, making it a true reversal. Alternatively, smaller and less active candlesticks that move in the reversal direction are less likely to stick as they are not carrying as much momentum, meaning that there is a good chance you will see the prices go back in the original direction again.

Bar Charts

Bar charts are more formally referred to as "open-high-low-close" or OHLC charts. These charts are the Western equivalent of the Japanese candlestick chart. Instead of looking like candlesticks the way the Japanese variation of the chart does, bar charts are reflected by vertical lines that have two small horizontal ticks on either side of the line, with the left tick being lower and the right tick being higher. These charts are read exactly the same as Japanese candlestick charts except for the fact that the bars do look slightly different and they do not alternate between green and red coloring.

The vertical line on the bar chart represents the overall price range of any given period. The top of the bar represents the highest price point for activity with that particular stock, whereas the bottom of the bar represents the lowest price point for activity with it. The range between the two horizontal ticks represents where the majority of trades were happening. The direction of the market itself will tell you which horizontal tick represents which price. Bars moving in a bullish direction are read with the lower tick reflecting the opening price and the upper tick reflecting the closing price. Bearish bars are read with the upper tick reflecting the opening price and the lower tick reflecting the closing price.

With bar charts, you cannot get quite as much detailed information from the chart itself as you can with candlestick charts, so most traders learn how to trade using Japanese candlestick charts instead. With that being said, understanding what the bar chart is and how it looks is important because there will be times that you are looking up information on stocks and there is information available on bar graphs. Knowing how to read them will ensure that this information makes sense to you and that you can apply it to the case you build around each stock that you are considering buying and selling.

Gaps

Price gaps occur on any form of the chart when the price of the stock changes overnight, or after hours, despite no one trading the stock during that period of time. Gaps generally only occur when a piece of news or specific events causes a flood of traders to either buy or sell the security, depending on what that news or event was.

For example, if a company were to launch a new product, you might find that their stocks jump overnight in anticipation for their increased value due to the stocks. Alternatively, if a company were to declare that they were filing for bankruptcy, you might see their stocks fall overnight. Either scenario can lead to a gap that results in the market changing from where it was during active trading hours. Gaps could indicate the start of a new trend, depending on what kind of gap it is and what triggered the gap to be started.

Chapter 9: Technical Analysis: Patterns

When you begin to read charts such as candlestick and bar charts, you are going to want to learn how to read patterns in those charts so that you can gain a strong understanding as to what is going on in the market. Certain patterns will indicate behaviors taking place in the market, as well as what is likely to happen next with the market. Tracking these trends can help you identify where the best trading opportunities lie, including where you should focus on entering and exiting positions in the market.

As a swing trader, there are five patterns you want to pay attention to in any market. These patterns include double bottoms and double tops, bear and bull pendants, bear and bull flags, ABCD patterns, and head and shoulder patterns. Each of these patterns has its own trading strategy, as you will learn about in this chapter.

Double Bottoms and Double Tops

Double bottoms and double tops are the most commonly traded pattern on candlestick charts as they provide straightforward information and tend to be fairly consistent in informing you as to how the market is about to behave. Double bottoms and double tops can be identified by seeing a market either drop or rise into the same position twice in a row, before reversing back into the opposite position. In fact, that is exactly what the double bottom and double top pattern prove: that the market is ready for a reversal.

This particular pattern appears almost every day in most stocks, yet identifying and trading on this pattern is not always the easiest thing to do. It can be challenging to anticipate when the pattern is swinging into action, making it difficult for you to determine where the best point of entry is going to be.

Traders have the choice of either anticipating this behavior by looking out for it in the market or to react to it as soon as it has happened. Anticipating it can be challenging because it requires you to have a strong understanding of what is going to happen in the market and if you are wrong you could lose out on quite a bit of money. However, reacting to it means that you are likely going to miss out on profits as well because you did not get in or out of your trade at the best possible opportunity, or at the peak of the bottom or top movement.

Bear and Bull Pennants

Pennants are a type of continuation pattern that can be identified by spotting large movements in a security that is followed by a consolidation period. During the consolidation period, the converging trend lines come together, which forms the pennant. The pennant is typically immediately followed by a breakout movement that will exist in the same direction as the original large movement direction occurred.

The pennant is similar to the flag structure, which we will discuss in the next section. They are viewable through the symmetrical triangle structure which essentially means that the market begins to rise and fall in equal amounts, creating a symmetrical triangle shame from the right side of your screen. When you see these pennants begin to take form, you can identify when the breakout will happen based on how close the pennant gets to the point of the symmetrical triangle. To create this visual, imagine drawing a symmetrical triangle at the right of your chart with two lines extending toward overbought and oversold market positions at the exact same angle. The movement of the trades inside moving back and forth evenly between these two triangle lines without ever breaking out of them. If they do, you have located a pennant. When the price starts to reach toward the triangles "point", you have found the breakout level, where the price is about to completely shift again.

For a pennant, the breakout will always head in the same direction that the market came into the pennant in. Bullish pennants enter the pennant pattern coming up from the bottom of your chart and heading toward the top, and will exit in this same direction. Bearish pennants enter the pattern coming down from the top of your chart and heading toward the bottom and will exit in the same direction.

If you want to trade these patterns, you need to enter the market when it reaches a low point in the bullish pennant, touching the bottom line of your symmetrical triangle. Then, you want to hold your position until the breakout occurs and reaches up beyond the high point of the start of the pennant. This is where you will be able to sell your stocks and secure your profits for your trade. You should set your stop loss at the lowest point of the first drop in the pennant to ensure that you can withstand a small amount of volatility before the market breaks out and reaches profit levels.

Bear and Bull Flags

Flags are a pattern that truly appears like flags on a flagpole when viewed on the charts. These patterns are identified by the development of a sharp countertrend, known as the flag, which is succeeded by a short-lived trend known as the flagpole. These patterns are found accompanied by representative volume indicators that help track the trend, as well as price action movements that define the pattern itself. When you see a flag pattern take place on a chart, you know that a trend reversal or breakout is about to happen, always following a period of consolidation.

Flag patterns are similar to pennants, but they are not identical. The movements of the flag do differ and what happens following a flag trend is also different. The flag trend can be identified by five separate characteristics that take place in this order: the preceding trend, the consolidation channel, the volume pattern, the breakout, and the confirmation. When all of these characteristics have played out, the pattern looks similar to a pennant except reversed. In this scenario, the tight "point" of the symmetrical triangle exists on the left side of the chart. The price action "opens" the triangle out further until it breaks out from the tug-of-war pattern and officially moves into a consistent direction. It is then followed by consistent movement in that direction for a few candlesticks to prove or "confirm" the pattern, ensuring that it has officially broken out and that it will continue moving in the new direction.

In a bullish flag pattern, the initial trend will include the price action rising, and then it will have a consistent declining direction during the consolidation period where the chart moves up and down fairly consistently. When the breakout happens, it will begin to move back into the bullish pattern where it will remain until a true reversal takes place and completely switches the direction of the stocks.

In a bearish flag pattern, the initial trend will include the price action falling and then there will be a consistent rise in price action during the consolidation period. When the breakout happens, the trend will move back into a consistent bearish position where it will remain until a true reversal takes place in the stock.

When you are trading on flag patterns, it can be challenging to know where to get in on the pattern to make your move. Like with double bottoms and double tops, there is a difficulty in deciding whether to act in anticipation or in response. If you act in anticipation and you are wrong, a true flag pattern may not complete itself and you may find yourself facing losses as the stock market heads for a true reversal. If, however, you act in reaction, you may be buying into a strong trend and minimizing or risking losing your overall profits from that trade.

As a beginner trader, the best thing to do is to trade in reaction to the market's movements but do so quickly. Look for the candlesticks that immediately confirm that the breakout has occurred, and then immediately buy into your position. Set your stop losses at the base of the last price drop to give the market some flexibility while also protecting yourself from losses. Your profit target should be set a few candlesticks ahead, at a price point that matches where you reasonably believe the market will rise to in the coming weeks.

ABCD Patterns

ABCD patterns are considered to be a basic harmonic pattern because they do not require a significant amount of volatility to be spotted, and they follow an excellent flow in the way they are laid out. Every other pattern that you see on the market is actually derived from the ABCD pattern which is the most basic pattern that you can follow.

The ABCD pattern consists of 3 price swings that take place. The AB and CD lines are identified as "legs", whereas the BC line that occurs in the center is known as the correction line. There are several ways that the ABCD pattern can look on the chart, including the fact that it can go either bullish or bearish depending on what is happening with the stock.

The rules for each pattern remain the same, no matter what the pattern itself actually looks like. In order for it to be a true ABCD pattern, the AB and CD lines need to be roughly the same size, and they need to be moving in the same direction. If you were to draw lines between the AB and CD lines back toward the BD crossing line, you should find that the two triangles created are roughly the same size and shape. They should have the same angles, meaning that it is moving in a true ABCD pattern.

When you see an ABCD pattern, it is crucial that you never enter the pattern until the price point reaches the "D" end of the CD line. In other words, it needs to reach the bottom of the third line in the pattern, when the price has already finished correcting and then falling once again. There are no special places for where you should put your stop loss on this trade, instead, you need to follow your own personal risk tolerance levels and place your stop loss accordingly.

Your profit target should be set around the point of the top of the correction or BC line, as this is where the market is most likely to reach back up to again. Although it may seem modest, it can still earn you a strong profit as long as the pattern proceeds as planned and is a strong position for you to hold.

Head and Shoulder Patterns

Head and shoulder patterns can be spotted on a chart when you see two peaks that are roughly the same height with one peak in the center that is much higher. Ideally, these head and shoulder patterns should occur at the overbought line with the peaks reaching well into the overbought market. You can test this by using an RSI or MACD indicator to see where the market is actually resting.

The reverse or inverted head and shoulder pattern is exactly the same, except flipped upside down and placed at the bottom of the chart into the oversold area of the market. The shoulders should still dip lower than the head dips, creating three peaks with the center one dropping the most. The shoulders should also drop about the same amount into this pattern for it to count as a true head and shoulders pattern.

You should never trade the head and shoulders pattern until the pattern is complete, otherwise, you may not be entering a true head and shoulders pattern. After it has completed, you can initiate your trade position by buying into your chosen part of the market. As a swing trader, you want to look for inverted head and shoulder patterns to buy into unless you are going to be trading options, in which case you can enter a put option during a true head and shoulders trade. (You can learn more about that in my other book, *Swing Trading Options*.)

Your stop losses should be placed just above the right shoulder of the pattern, and your profit targets should be placed at the price difference between the head and low point of either shoulder in the trade.

Chapter 10: Swing Trading with Tools and Indicators

Applying all of the knowledge that you have learned to actually swing trade using the tools and indicators we have already discussed can be somewhat intimidating. You may be feeling a small amount of information overload at this point, as you attempt to identify how it all comes together to create one flawless trading system. Although it all makes sense right now in individual pieces, you want to make sure that you put everything together in a way that is going to make sense and support you with making the best trades possible.

When it comes to trading, you want to make sure that you are always following the most direct, straightforward approach to everything you do. Your entire strategy and system should make sense, should not contain any unnecessary "fluff" and should support you in making the best trades possible. We are going to start putting those pieces together now by taking a look into how swing trading works when you are actively using the tools and indicators that we have talked about so far. This way, you understand not only what these tools and indicators are, but how they work and how you can use them to support your trades.

How to Use Moving Averages

Moving averages help you get a feel for how the stock is moving, in general, over any given period of time, and they can be incredibly helpful in connecting you with the information you need to predict the market and plan trades. Basic moving averages can be set to cover any period of time, with shorter time periods making the moving average line far more sensitive than longer time periods. For example, a 200-period line is going to be a lot more gradual and will be less likely to track volatility in the market, whereas a 15-period line is going to be far more sensitive and will track the volatility over that period more closely.

The best way to use moving average lines effectively is to place two moving average lines; one with a shorter time period and one with a longer time period. How long you want these time periods to be will depend on what type of trading you are engaging in. With swing trading, you want to use fairly short time periods, with a 15-MA and a 50-MA. This means that the moving average line will track 15-period and 50-period timeframes, respectively. The two lines are going to both be quite sensitive, although the 15-MA line will be much more sensitive as it tracks a shorter time frame in the market, and therefore, it tracks the volatility a little closer.

In order to use moving averages to identify support in a strong trading position, you want to see both MA lines moving toward the same direction by the end of the chart. Ideally, they should both be moving bullish if you are preparing to buy into the market and they should both be moving bearish if you are preparing to exit the market.
If they are not moving in the same direction at the point where you are looking to trade, you need to wait until they flow together. MAs that are moving in opposite directions indicate volatility and could indicate the possible reversal of the short-term and long-term trading trends.

Tips for Using Tools Effectively

Using all of your tools, such as moving averages, indicators, charts, news platforms, stock analysis platforms, technical analysis software, and anything else you have chosen to use in trading is valuable. With that being said, you need to make sure that you are using your tools appropriately to prevent yourself from wasting time and putting yourself at risk with your tools. In learning how to use your tools properly, you are going to strengthen your skills as a trader, improve the quality of your trades, and maximize your profits.

Validate the Quality of Your Tools

Before you ever begin using any tool for trading, you should always first make sure that the tools you are using are high quality. There are many trading tools and resources for knowledge out there, many of which are not going to be able to offer you the quality of tools or knowledge that you need in order to improve your trades. Using low-quality tools or gaining information from low-quality resources can lead you experiencing a complete flop in your trades because the information you have based your trade on is low quality.

In general, any tool you use should be easy to understand, easy to use, and known for being accurate and reliable. Ideally, you should look for many recommendations on what tools to use to ensure that you are using the best ones possible. You should also consider using 2-3 different tools for any one given area of your trading so that you can cross-check information across these tools. The tools should all generally say the same thing, and if they do, this should be used as a positive influence in helping you decide what your next trade move will be.

News and informational resource platforms should also be thoroughly checked for quality. Some news platforms out there are known for waiting for news to release from top-rated platforms, and then release the same information a little bit later on their own platforms.

These platforms are not necessarily the best to follow because you could find yourself late to the information. You also want to make sure the information being shared consistently checks out as true and helpful. Any platforms that are sharing information that is inconsistent, unclear, or even completely false should be avoided as they may lead to you taking on poor information for your trades.

Do Not Rely On Any One Tool

Whenever you are using trading tools, you should refrain from relying on any one single tool for your trades. While there are strategies that you should use which primarily rely on one single tool, you should still use other tools to validate your decisions to ensure that you are making the best trade decisions possible.

Ideally, you should see your theory being validated by every tool you do use to ensure that you are entering the best trade. However, if you are seeing one or two tools showing conflicting information, that does not necessarily mean that all of the information coming from all of the other tools is not right. Instead, you need to verify where that information is coming from and determine how much it will impact your risk exposure in the trade.

For example, if all of your indicators are suggesting that everything is optimal for you to enter a trade but the fundamental analysis of a company shows otherwise or new news surfaces that strongly suggests otherwise, it may be better to sit that trade out. Diversify where you get your information from and ensure that you always consider the priority of the information you are receiving before entering trades.

Do Not Overwhelm Yourself With the Tools You Are Using

Although you do want to cross-reference the information you gain to ensure that you are getting the best information possible, you do not want to overwhelm yourself with too much information because this can detract from the quality of your trade. Using too many different tools is the same as obsessively checking news reports and stock analysis charts to make sure your trade is going well: it is overwhelming and it invokes fear. Fear is never a trader's ally, so you want to avoid behaviors that invoke fear.

With that being said, you should limit yourself to only using 2-3 different tools in any given category to validate and verify the quality of your trades. For example, you might use 2-3 indicators, 2-3 news sources, 2-3 technical analysis software, and so forth to ensure that you are accumulating enough information to build your case, but not obsessing over every little detail. Overall, these tools should be increasing your confidence in your trade, not overwhelming you or feeding into any fear you might have around the trade.

Take Your Time Understanding How Each Tool Works

Before you begin to trade using any new tool, you should always take your time in understanding how each new tool works. For example, you should focus on learning what an indicator looks like, how it follows the market, and how to read patterns in that indicator before you attempt to use it in active trade. You should also take your time to educate yourself on what the strategies for each indicator are, and how to plan those strategies and execute them before you get started.

Using practice trades can be a wonderful opportunity for you to learn how to use those tools in action before you actually put any money into your trade. In this scenario, you would use your trading journal and plot down the exact moment you would enter the market based on this indicator and why. You would also pretend to manage the trade and then exit using the indicator's information, while also writing down what you are doing, how, and why. After 1-2 practices trades with an indicator, you should feel more confident in understanding how it works in live-action so that you can begin to use it in real trades.

Use Your Indicators to Validate Trades, Not To Spot Them

The indicators that you use in trading should always be used to validate trends, not spot them. You should be spotting trends using chart analysis, news on reliable stock platforms, and fundamental analysis to help you spot where your best trades should be positioned. Once you have identified possible locations, you should be using tools to validate these trends and verify the quality of the trades. Attempting to use indicators to spot trends can be overwhelming because each indicator looks slightly different and will provide you with slightly different information.

If you are not already somewhat confident in the quality of a trade, you should not use a tool like an indicator to try and build your confidence. Alternatively, if you use indicators and validate a trade but you still feel underconfident in that trade, you should also consider passing it up. Any time you do not feel truly confident in a trade, even if that trade were to be high quality your own emotional influence could result in you having a poor experience in that position.

Always Look Long Term, Even When Planning Short Positions

Whenever you are planning out a trade, you should always use your tools to look into the long-term position of that trade. While it is never advised to stay in a trade longer than you plan to, it is important to know that the trends of the market are likely to stay in favor longer than you plan on being in the trade for. Attempting to enter a trade and stay in until the very last minute before the trend drops, especially if you have not done enough research to know that the drop is coming, can be dangerous. If the market is anticipated to reverse too close to the end of your trade, that drop could come sooner than anticipated and result in a loss for you. Always look into the long-term position and trade as if you were staying in the position long term to ensure that you are protecting your position and not entering something with too much risk.

Make Use of Every Risk Management Tool You Have

On the topic of risk: always make sure that every trade you make has all of your risk management tools applied to it. The primary ones for trading are stop losses and profit targets. Always apply your stop losses and profit targets to your trades to ensure that you are not engaged in an open, high-risk trade. Anytime you fail to set these risk management tools in place, you are trading ignorantly and are exposing yourself to massive losses. You should always have your stop losses and profit target positions planned out in advance so that the minute you enter a trade, you can set your stop loss and then your profit target, effectively protecting you while you are in your position.

Chapter 11: Swing Trading Strategies

Now that you have some of the basics down, let's dig even deeper and get into some strategies for how you can trade using the various technical indicators that we discussed in Chapter 6. These strategies are going to help you not only understand what these indicators are telling you, but also determine what the best method is for using this information to develop a trading plan.

Ichimoku Kinko Hyo (Ichimoku Cloud) Strategies

Trading the Ichimoku requires you to primarily focus on the cloud, which you may recall as being the two indicators that extending into the future trade positions. These two indicators are the senkou span A and senkou span B lines, and the space between them is known as the Ichimoku "cloud".

In order to trade with the Ichimoku, you want to identify the cloud and then use the Tenkan and Kijun Sen lines to help you determine what is presently going on in the market. Remember, the Tenkan line is the moving average and then Kijun Sen is the baseline that lets you know the base price for that particular stock. You want to pay attention to what is happening with these two lines to identify what is likely going to happen to the stock prices as they continue maturing. Ideally, they should continue moving into the cloud and should indicate positive flow for you to trade into.

To spot a bullish market, you want to look for the moment the Tenkan rises over the Kijun Sen line, which means the price is likely going to increase. At this point, the cloud should exist in a positive bullish direction for the market. To spot a bearish market, the Tenkan should drop below the Kijun Sen line, which means the price is likely going to decrease. In this scenario, the cloud should exist in a bearish range going forward. Upon spotting where the market is, you want to buy into it when it is bullish and sell out when it is going bearish, naturally.

To time your purchase with the Ichimoku, you want to buy your stocks slightly above the cloud barrier's bottom line, or the senkou span B line. This is your best opportunity to get into the market before the trend runs too deep and you miss out on your profitable position. Your stop loss should be placed just above the high point of the first candle within the cloud formation to ensure that you do not drop below a reasonable point in your trade. You want to place your profit target wherever you reasonably feel the market will rise to, however, placing one around halfway up the cloud is typically ideal. This way, you are likely to reach that profit target and it should not take too terribly long for you to get there.

Bollinger Band Strategies

When you are trading with Bollinger bands, you want to use the upper and lower bands as price targets, which enables you to get a sense of what to expect with the market. If you see the prices touch or pass the upper line, you know the stock has been overbought. Likewise, if you see them touch or pass the lower line, you know the stock has been oversold. As someone who is looking to buy into trades, you want to look for the market to drop under the lower line of the Bollinger band, which triggers a buy signal.

Upon entering a buying position with a Bollinger band, the upper line represents where profits are expected to rise back up toward. However, just because this is expected does not mean that it will happen. For that reason, you do not want to set your profit target up exactly on that upper line.

Instead, you want to set it a few bars below where that line would reach, as the market usually trades within 3-4 bars below the upper line of the Bollinger band.

This way, you are setting profit targets that are likely to be reached rather than ones that are too greedy for what you are likely to achieve from your trades. With that being said, your stop loss should be placed 1-2 candlesticks above the lower band so that you have some tolerance room for the volatility of the market.

Parabolic Stop and Reverse (SAR) Strategies

The best strategy to use with the parabolic SAR is to actually use it alongside other indicators. This indicator pairs well with the ADX, in particular, because they both work together to identify the direction and momentum of the stocks being traded. This indicator should be used primarily as a strategy for identifying where your stop losses should be placed on your orders to give yourself room for volatility without risking massive losses.

As soon as you see the indicator switch into the bearish position, where the dots exist above the candles instead of below them, you want to place a stop loss. The stop loss should be placed to match the level of the indicator after every price bar on the chart.

If you want to use the parabolic SAR exclusively, you should seek to buy into a trade when the indicator switches from being placed over candles to being placed under. When you see this switch happen, it means the general direction of the market is changing and you can get yourself placed for those changes.

As soon as you see the indicator switch back into the opposite position, you should sell your stocks. Although it may not be a long-term drop, it is an indicator that prices are going to start dropping and if you exit now you can maintain your profits.

Relative Strength Index (RSI) Strategies

Trading with the RSI is simple. You want to place this indicator onto your chart and watch for patterns that are taking place in the chart. As soon as you see the stock dip into the 0-30% frame at the bottom of the screen, you want to buy into those stocks as they are due for a correction. You should place your stop loss 2-3 candlesticks below where you bought in so that you can endure a little further overselling before the market corrects itself.

Then, you should place your profit target at a point that makes reasonable sense to the market itself. If the stock has been largely volatile and consistently swinging back and forth from overbought to oversold, chances are you can set your profit targets a bit higher and still achieve those targets. If, however, you notice the stock has been dipping into oversold a few times over before switching back, or gradually moving in any one direction, you are going to want to pick a lower more modest profit target for your trade. This way, your greed does not cost you profits in the end.

The RSI can be used with other momentum indicators like the MACD indicator to verify what you have discovered with the RSI. This way, you feel confident that what you have discovered is indeed true and you buy in at the best opportunities and sell at the best opportunities, too.

When trading the RSI with the MACD, you want to look for the RSI to drop into oversold and the MACD to show a divergence away from the price to prove that the market is going to move in favor of you earning profits. This way, you are more likely to earn profits from your trade. As well, you can use the MACD to help indicate where your profit targets should be set for that trade, enabling you to create even stronger parameters around your trades.

Moving Average Convergence Divergence (MACD) Strategies

The MACD indicator is one that can give you fairly reliable information as to when trends are going to switch into a reversal based on where the lines are positioned with each other. When the blue line rises above the red line, this indicates that the market is in a bullish position, whereas when it falls below the red line, this indicates the market is in a bearish position. You want to track these two lines to get a sense for where the market is heading, which will help you determine your entry and exit points for the market.

Ideally, you want to follow the indicator, and as soon as you see the lines cross into a bullish market, you want to time your entry. You should place your stop loss at the very bottom of tail of the current candlestick at that point, which should give you plenty of room for volatility. Then, you should place your profit target around halfway up the difference between the space of the divergence lines.

Average Directional Index Strategies

Before you begin using the ADX to develop a strategy, you should read the price point on the chart, first. This is the most important information above anything else. Once you have read the price action on the chart, you can read the ADX to get context around what the price is doing, and why it is doing it. You are likely going to notice that the best trends will rise out of periods of consolidation in the price points, so you want to look for these periods of consolidation, and then look for breakouts. When you see breakout trends, this generally means that the period of consolidation is over.

Based on the nature of the ADX, it is ideal to use this to reinforce what you have learned about a price using another trading indicator, such as the RSI. By combining the information you find from the two, you can feel confident that you are timing your entry and exit points to the best of your ability and maximizing your profits in each trade.

Stochastic Strategies

Finding trading strategies for the stochastic indicator is virtually identical to finding trading strategies for RSI. With this indicator, you want to look for markets that have been oversold to buy into, and markets that have been overbought to sell out of. You can track these trends by watching for the line on the indicator to drop below 20, and over 80. When you see a crossover in these ranges, they serve as strong signals that it is a great time for you to engage in trading or exit your position.

When you trade with the stochastic indicator, it is important to pay attention to individual stock patterns. Each stock is going to have different behaviors based on what that stock is and how people like to trade it. You want to track these patterns to get an idea for how long it is likely to be before the stock reaches back into an overbought position. If it is going to be too long, naturally, you should place your profit target at a more modest price that you are more likely to reach into. If it is going to be relatively quick, you may be able to set your profit targets higher and still reach them in a reasonable amount of time.

OBV: On-Balance Volume Strategies

In order to trade with OBV, you first need to understand the OBV's relationship to closing prices between two successful trading days. The OBV indicates a positive trading opportunity when the second day's price closes above the closing price of the day prior.

When the second day's price closes higher than the price of the first day, you calculate the OBV using the following equation: (OBV = Previous OBV + Current trading volume). If the price closes higher on the first day than it does on the second day, the OBV is calculated using this equation instead: (OBV = Previous OBV − Current Trading Volume). The real OBV of any given stock relies on the starting date of the trade, as it does not change as frequently as other indicators do.

When you are preparing to get into a trade, you want to see that the OBV is steadily increasing day over day, as this proves that the overall market is heading in a positive direction. In this case, the OBV would serve as a good support indicator to another indicator like the RSI or the Ichimoku to create a trading entry point. If the OBV is decreasing day over day, this would indicate that it is time to exit a trade to avoid incurring any unwanted losses from the trade that you are currently in.

Elliott Wave Analysis

The Elliott wave theory was made by Ralph Nelson Elliott and is used to describe price movements in financial markets. In these financial markets, Elliott observed recurring fractal wave patterns that can be identified in both stock and consumer behavior relating to the stock market. In order to trade using the Elliott wave analysis strategy, you want to look for waves taking place in the market. These waves will look a lot like the ABCD patterns described in Chapter 9, except that you will see multiple occurring and they will be increasing in overall value or decreasing in overall value.

There are two types of waves that exist in the Elliott wave theory: impulsive waves and corrective waves. The impulsive waves refer to the waves that are generally increasing in value indicating a volatile bullish market. The corrective waves refer to the waves that are generally decreasing in value indicating a volatile bearish market. Looking for these waves in the market can help you identify general market trends, as well as volatility in the market itself. As a swing trader, a highly volatile market with many Elliott waves present is actually a positive sign, as this means there are plenty of strong swings for you to get into in order to help you make a profit.

Your strategy with the Elliot wave theory should be to validate the waves using another indicator, like the ADX indicator or the OBV indicator to ensure that the market is still steadily moving in a positive direction for you. At that point, you want to identify a swing in the market and place your entry into the market at that swing. Then, you want to place your stop loss at the bottom tail of that candlestick to ensure that you do not incur any major losses. Your profit target should be set in accordance with the volatility of the market itself to ensure that you earn your desired profits.

Chapter 12: Swing Trading: Vital Guidelines and Suggestions

In order to become the most effective trader possible, you need to follow vital guidelines and important suggestions to help you improve your skills and become a better trader. These strategies are not necessarily going to impact each individual trade you enter like risk management strategies might, but they are going to help you set yourself up for much stronger trades. Most experienced traders use these as a means to create rules for themselves around how they are going to trade and how they are going to improve their skills to become better traders. Following them can improve your skills, too.

Set Effective Trading Goals

One of the best things you can do for yourself is to learn how to set an effective goal that relates to what you desire to achieve with trading. Having effective goals in place as a trader can keep you focused, help you decide what trades to enter, and give you an idea around how you should manage your profits and money in general with trading. All of this is achieved through goal setting because having a goal gives you a sense of direction and a means of determining what is right and what is wrong for you personally.

As a trader, there are five types of trade goals you should be making for yourself in order to give yourself something to work toward, as well as a strong sense of direction in the market. These goals include a personal goal, risk control goals, effort to reward ratio goals, reviewing goals, and profit goals.

Your personal goal defines why you are trading and what you seek to achieve as a trader. This is where you get to decide what you want to spend your profit on, which can be anything you truly desire in your life. You might be looking to replace your income, retire early, travel, send your kids to college, or do any other number of things that will require you to have increased capital in your life. Whatever your goal is, make it something personal and meaningful so that you are more likely to work toward it in your life.

Your risk control goal is a goal that you should set that ultimately outlines the fact that you are going to seek to control your risk in every trade that you enter. This means that you are not going to enter any trade that has any unknown risk, that you are not going to enter trades without setting your risk management tools, and that you are going to do all that you can to minimize risk in every way possible.

Your effort to reward ratio is the ratio that determines how much effort you would actually have to put into a trade in order to earn profits from that trade. Some trades, such as those that have incredibly high volatility, are ones that will require far too much effort on your behalf to enter and maintain your position in order to maximize your profits.

The best thing to do is have a goal in place that determines how much of an effort you are willing to put in so that you can profit, and never go beyond that effort level. Entering trades that will require too much effort can leave you at risk because you may not have the time or energy to put into that effort and make your profits. Stick to trades that match your effort to ratio goal.

Your reviewing goal is a simple goal that determines that you are going to review every single trade you make to see how you excelled and what you could have done to improve that trade. These are important goals as they help you ensure that you are always working toward your best in each trade. Turning this into a goal means you are more likely to stick to your reviewing habit, which means you are more likely to improve over time.

Profit goals are another important goal to have, as they give you the opportunity to determine how much profit you want to earn per trade. You should set a goal for what percentage of increase you want to see from each trade, and then you should refuse to trade anything that goes too far below or above that profit to avoid wasting your time and energy on a trade or exposing yourself to risk.

Create Trading Objectives

Trading objectives are like goals, but they are what you desire to achieve with each individual trade. Before you go into any given trade position you have considered, measure that trade position against your goals to determine whether or not it fits in with what you are trying to achieve as a trader. If you find that it does not match your goals, you should skip that trade to avoid going against what you are trying to achieve. If it does match your goals, you can go ahead and enter that trade.

Before you do officially enter a trade, make sure that you set a goal around how you want it to go. In fact, you should set three goals: the worst-case scenario, the good, the great goals. Having all of these goals in sight ensure that you know exactly what your strategy is, how you are going to achieve that strategy, and how that trade will rank depending on how it behaves.

Your worst-case scenario is what would happen if you were to take a loss. This should outline where you are going to set your stop losses, effectively making your stop loss the "worst-case scenario." For example, if you are purchasing a stock at $1 per share and your stop-loss is fixed at $0.90 per share, then your worst-case scenario would be that you lose $0.10 per share. Obviously, this is not a goal that you want to achieve because you would rather profit, but instead, this is a goal about minimizing your risk and losses.

Your good and great goals should both be set at different ranking positions for profits that you could earn from your trade deal. Your great goal is where your profit target should be placed, and it should be a realistic goal for the profits you want to earn from your trade. Your great goal is ultimately what you are going for and it is the reason why you are entering this trade in the first place. This goal has your desired profit margins fixed in place and will offer you enough profits to make it worth the effort.

Your good goal is a backup goal of sorts. This goal is rarely ever activated because you plan on hitting your great goal every time. However, sometimes, the market does not do what we expect it will do and we are not going to achieve that great goal. Accepting this reality is an important part of trading. By accepting this, you can set a "good" goal which defines where you will exit the market if it seems like you are not reaching your great goal this time around. This way, you still profit at a reasonable level and you are able to move on to your next trade.

Build A Daily Schedule

Having a daily schedule is an important part of being a great trader. A daily schedule affords you the ability to continually follow the same rituals and routines that will support you with completing every trade. Having the same routines in place for everything you do ensures that you never miss a step due to chaos or disorganization, which would be a trader's nightmare.

Every trader needs to have a schedule in place, and all experienced traders have one that they have been using since day one. Your schedule may expand and grow over the years, but the primary goal is to have a schedule that you can continue to follow every single day for the rest of your trading career. The only time your schedule should be adjusted is if at any point in your learning either from others or from reviewing your own practices you realize that a shift in your schedule could increase your profitability. In this case, you should adapt your schedule. Otherwise, you want to keep it the same every day as often as possible.

The general schedule that every trader follows is typically the same. The day is broken down into pre-market, early trading, second wind, and post-market sections to identify what the trader needs to be doing at every point throughout their day.

The pre-market is when a trader wakes up, checks in on the markets, and starts planning out the day ahead. At this point, your goal is to manage your stocks by seeing how they have performed overnight, while also finding new possible positions for you to enter in the market. The new possible positions should all go on a watchlist that you will use to track these stocks and ultimately identify your best positions, which should be done right before the market opens. Finding the exact positions you will take should be done using proper technical analysis so that you know exactly where you are going to enter the minute the market opens.

The early trading and second wind portions of the market are where you exercise your strategies. This is where you are going to actually enter those positions and open up some trade deals. Passive traders or part-time traders will generally only trade on the early trading part of the market, whereas those who want to trade full time or professionally will trade both parts of the market. If you are trading on the second wind, as soon as you enter your positions that you determined during pre-market hours, you should start looking for more positions.

The post-market time is where you track your daily trade deals and review how your day went. This is your opportunity to recall every single trade you made with each trade fresh in your mind and identify how you did great and where you could have done better. Keep note of these pieces of information so that you can apply it as you go forward, ensuring that each trade always sees you improving your skills just a little bit further.

Commit to Learning More Daily

Lastly, every single trader should commit to learning more about trading every single day. This should come from more than just your own trading journals, but also from other resources. There are plenty of resources out there that traders can use to help create a stronger understanding of how trading works and how they can improve their own trading skills.

Some of the best resources you can look into for learning more every day are books and YouTube channels that are devoted to teaching people about trading. Again, make sure that you are always purchasing materials that are of high quality and that are known for having reliable information within to ensure that you are getting the best information possible. The more that you can learn and educate yourself on the market, the more confident you are going to feel in it and the more effectively you are going to be able to trade in future trades. Education truly will help deepen your understanding of the market and your intuition around how it works. It is worth it to invest at least 20-30 minutes every single day to reading or listening to how to trade the markets to become the best trader possible, even if you only plan on trading part-time or passively.

Chapter 13: How to Trade Different Financial Instruments

The final element you need to know about swing trading is the different financial instruments that you can trade with. Swing trading itself is just a strategy for how you are going to position yourself in the market, so it does not indicate exactly what you are going to be trading. This means that you can decide to trade whatever you want to trade on the market from the range of financial instruments that are available for you. In general, there are five financial instruments people will trade using swing trading: ETFs, options, stocks, crypto, and forex. We will discuss all of those here so that you can identify what financial instrument is going to be best for you.

Swing Trading ETF: Pros and Cons

ETFs are a form of security that can be invested in or traded. As a swing trader, you will be trading ETFs which means that you will essentially be trading a small "basket" of stocks and bonds that have been pre-selected by the ETF manager. Investors are the ones who place funds into the ETF for it to be developed and traded in the first place.

The pros of trading ETFs is that they are low cost and efficient. They also tend to be more reliable for traders to get into because they are not typically quite as volatile and are considered to be low-risk investments in general. Plus, based on the way they are structured, they can be openly traded on any exchange.

The biggest con of trading ETFs is that they are popularly traded by other traders, which results in them being a "hot stock". When traders get into the scene of trading ETFs, they realize how easy it is and it can be simple to try to chase a hot trend, only to find yourself losing out in the end. If traders get too much invested in ETFs exclusively and nothing else, they can take on massive losses over time that may exceed their profits.

Swing Trading Options: Pros and Cons

Options are a financial instrument that is made up of contracts that represent the right to a certain stock at a certain price by a certain date. Each option contract is made up to represent 100 shares of a certain stock, and in the contract is a strike price and an expiry date. The strike price reflects how much the stock will be bought or sold for if the option is exercised on or before the expiry date. Depending on the type of option a trader buys, they either purchase the right to buy or sell the stock or the option to buy or sell stock at the strike price.

The pro of options is that they are low investments and that they do provide a massive hedge against risk in the market. If you buy an option, you can purchase the right to buy or sell stock at one price but wait until the market confirms itself before actually taking action. This is the biggest reason why people trade options, because of the risk protection.

The con of trading stocks is that they do have expiry dates, which means that if they are not exercised by a specific date, the contract is null or worthless as we call it in trading. If the contract expires worthless, the trader is out whatever they paid on the premium of the contract in order to purchase it in the first place. Another drawback is that the options market does not represent all of the stocks on the open market, so you will not be able to trade every security with options. Instead, you will only be able to trade some of them, and sometimes, those ones can be rather volatile and challenging to trade which is largely the reason as to why they have options in the first place.

Swing Trading Stocks: Pros and Cons

Stocks are what we have used as the primary financial instrument in this book to describe various strategies and trading opportunities. Stocks represent shares in a company, meaning that when you buy stocks, you technically own a very tiny percentage of the company that you are trading stocks in. Buying and selling stocks is one of the most common trading strategies and it tends to be what people automatically think about anytime they think of trading.

The pro of trading stocks is that they are the best way to earn maximum profits. With stocks, you are directly in the most volatile market which means that you have access to huge price increases that you will directly profit from. Plus, companies are always releasing new news and information around their business that causes fluctuations in prices which means that there are always plenty of great trading opportunities coming available.

The con of stocks happens to be one of the same reasons it is such a great trading commodity: it's volatility. Volatility, especially for a swing trader, means that you have plenty of opportunities to trade stocks. However, it also means that the market is unpredictable and there is no way to know for sure what direction the market is going to go next, even if you have charted the patterns and performed your analysis on the market. For that reason, even if you are absolutely confident that you are going to earn profits from your trade, there is always the chance that you could miss out on them, leading to losses instead.

Swing Trading Crypto: Pros and Cons

Crypto, short for cryptocurrency, is another trading style that can be done on the market. Trading crypto is similar to trading currency, which essentially means that you are buying and selling stocks of crypto. When you are trading crypto, there are two options: you can trade the currency itself or shares of the company that invented and manages the crypto.

The benefit of trading crypto is that it is flexible with many ways to enter a market. You can buy into a market with CFDs, or contract for difference, which behaves similarly to an option. Or, you can buy into a market directly. By using either strategy, you can trade on short or long positions enabling you to conduct whatever trade strategy you desire with crypto including swing trading. Another benefit of crypto is that it is volatile which means that there are many opportunities for swing trades to be completed. Also, they provide you with great leverage which means that you can potentially trade them for even higher levels of profit as long as you are trading properly, and aware that you will be exposing yourself to higher losses too.

The cons of trading crypto are that this trading strategy is not perfect. There are some serious downfalls that can be faced, especially if you are not managing your trades properly. These downfalls largely fall around volatility, as these stocks can be highly volatile. Also, brokerages tend to charge higher amounts to trade crypto which means that you are more likely to lose out on bottom line profits because of how much you have invested in being able to trade the spread at all. Lastly, the crypto market is still largely unregulated and so are cryptocurrencies themselves. This can lead to a lot of uncertainty around the market which can result in strange breakouts and trends in the market, and which in and of themselves pose a risk. For example, the market could technically get shut down at any point with no warning due to unclear regulation standards around it. As well, you need to look at your own countries regulation as the exact regulations around it vary from country to country.

Swing Trading Forex: Pros and Cons

Forex is short for foreign exchange, and it is one of the most popularly traded global markets in the world. This exchange represents currencies that exist all around the world. The forex is a 24/7 exchange that has easy accessibility and that is traded professionally by many traders. Many traders will become professional traders from the comfort of their own homes where they can make money from their mobile phone or laptop by accessing the exchange through their brokerage and trading there. Many young graduates and even experienced professionals trade forex, and so do many who simply educate themselves from private resources and choose to get started.

The benefits of forex are that the market itself does tend to have very low costs. Both brokerage and commission fees tend to be lows, and there are no real commissions in the market because most brokers are profiting from the spreads between forex currencies. The benefit of this is that there are typically no separate charges associated with trading forex, which makes the experience very straightforward. Another benefit is that the market suits various trading styles from short-term traders to long-term traders, and those who want to trade using any strategy that exists. Also, the market has a high liquidity rate which means that you can easily cash out and take your profits at any time. While this is possible in any market, forex is known for being an easy place to rapidly sell of your stocks if you so desire so that you can earn larger profits from your trades.

The cons about trading on forex vary, with one of the more prominent ones being a lack of transparency. The forex market is deregulated, which means that it is largely dominated by brokers that have been known to trade against professionals. With a broker-dominated field, a trader may not know how their trade is being fulfilled, which could lead to him not getting the best price or getting limited views on their trading quotes as they are only selected by his broker. Another drawback is that the price determination process is complex, so it can be challenging for traders to understand exactly why and how certain trades are being calculated. Finally, the market is highly volatile which can be a great thing but it can also be a drawback, depending on what part of the market you are in. In some cases, sticking to regular stocks over forex is a better solution as the prices are somewhat easier to calculate and gauge and are more transparent than those on the forex.

Conclusion

Swing trading is a great strategy for any trader to enter, regardless of what their trading goals are. If you want to have the capacity to earn significant profits without having to wait so long to get them or endure the stress of day-to-day volatility quite so much, swing trading is the trading strategy for you.

This trading strategy is known for being one of the best strategies for beginners and experienced traders alike, as it has so many benefits to it. As well, there is so much that people can frequently learn from this strategy. It can take ages to master, yet you can still earn a huge profit from day one so long as you trade properly and follow the right strategies to keep yourself profitable.

After finishing this book, I strongly encourage you to engage in some practice trades before trying anything serious. Take out your trading book, take the knowledge you have learned here, and start going through your day as if you are truly trading. Create your watchlist, read the market and your indicators, time your entries, manage your practice trades, and time your exits. As you do, go through this book all over again, applying the knowledge to your practice trades along the way.

Once you begin to feel confident in practice trading, you can begin to engage in real trades. At this point, you will have a strong level of confidence behind you that will support you in staying out of a fear mindset when it comes to trading. Just make sure you do not switch into a greed mindset as this would not be ideal and could cost you big time. Instead, stay humble and confident in what you are doing and maintain a healthy respect for the market.

After a few real trades, you will find that trading is not nearly as challenging or as intimidating as people make it out to be. While it certainly does have challenges and learning curves, it is something that anyone can do and that anyone can profit from. Plenty of people are earning consistent profits off of the market and creating strong incomes for themselves using these strategies, which means you can absolutely do it, too.

The final piece of advice I want to leave you with is to be serious about keeping your trading journals. Trading journals are going to help you track charts, patterns, prices, and positions in the market while also tracking your own improvements. Every trader can benefit from keeping journals and keeping them organized, so do not overlook this trading tip. Also, make sure that you review your trade journals every so often so that you can recall all of the tips you have learned along the way as writing them down only to forget them would not be helpful!

Lastly, if you have enjoyed reading *Swing Trading for Beginners: The 2019/20 Valuable Swing Trading Tips In This Ultimate Guide You Will Learn How to Improve Your Trading Results and Your Finances with the Best Low-Risk Application* and feel that it has supported you in learning about swing trading or becoming a better swing trader, I ask that you please review it. Your honest feedback would be greatly appreciated.

Thank you, and best of luck!

Terminology

The stock market comes with its own terminology and jargon. Learning how to read and understand this jargon will help you understand what you are learning about and doing in the market.

Annual Report

An annual report is a report that companies provide that issues a significant amount of information regarding that company, ranging from cash flow to management strategy. All of the information in this report will affect the stock value of that company in one way or another. Annual reports are relevant to fundamental analysis.

Bear Market

A bear market is a trading term that represents a market that is moving into a downtrend or where the prices are decreasing. If a stock begins to fall, it is a bearish stock in a bear market.

Bull Market

A bull market is a trading term that represents a market that is moving into an uptrend or where the prices are increasing. If a stock begins to rise, it is a bullish stock in a bull market.

Broker

A broker is a person who buys or sells investments for you in exchange for a fee. Online brokerages are companies who give you access to the exchange.

Close

Close is the time that the stock market closes and is also used to reflect the closing price of a stock or the price that it is when the market closes.

Exchange

Exchange is a place in which different investments are traded. This is where traders get access to the market itself to conduct their trades, which is typically accessed through their online brokerages.

Execution

Execution means that the trading strategy has been completed or executed.

Leverage

Leverage means that you borrow shares in stock from your broker, and then you leverage those funds to increase your profits. It is important to understand that this leverage is a loan so you have to pay it back, plus interest on the leverage. If you lose your leverage due to bad trades, you are now indebted to your brokerage and have to pay from your own capital.

Moving Average

A moving average is the average price-per-share for any given stock during a specific period of time specified by the trader themselves. You can decide what time period you want to look at to gain your average.

Sector

A sector is a group of stocks that belong to the same industry. An example of a sector would be the technology sector in which stocks like Microsoft and Apple are traded.

Volatility

Volatility refers to the price movements of a stock, although it can also refer to a specific sector of the stock market or even the stock market as a whole. Stocks that are highly volatile have a large amount of back-and-forth price action, whereas stocks that are not as volatile have lower price action movements.

Volume

Volume represents the number of shares of a stock that is being traded at any given time. Typically, the volume is measured over a day-to-day time period.

Disclaimer

Please note that *Swing Trading for Beginners,* Jim Livermore, and anyone related to creating this book are not to be held liable for any results that the reader may gain from trading using these strategies. This book is designed for educational purposes only and should be viewed as such by the reader. Any action the reader takes on the information in this book is solely the responsibility and liability of the reader themselves, no one else.

My FREE Gift for You

At the time of writing this book, I also wrote an excellent book called *Swing Trading Options*. If you purchase that book to expand your knowledge in swing trading and to become a better trader, I will give you a gift of 2 Swing Trading Audiobooks 100% FREE.

Swing Trading Options is an excellent book that features everything you need to know about swing trading options, ranging from what options are and how they work to how to apply swing trading strategies to options specifically. I highly recommend Swing Trading options for Beginners and experienced traders alike, as it is an excellent way to earn strong profits while also hedging yourself against risk.

What Should I Read Next?

Swing Trading Option: The Ultimate Trading Guide to Discover Safe and Profitable Trading Strategies for Generating Fast and Secure Profits and Rapid Growth for Your Finances

Stocks Option Trading: Learn and Understand How Everything Works and What Pitfalls you MUST Avoid as a Beginner. Learn How Top Investors Lower Their Cost Basis Using Stock Options

Stock Options Trading Strategies: The Best Step-by-Step Guide to Learn How to Trade Stocks and Discover How TOP Traders Invest. The Best Strategies to Help You Create Your Financial Freedom

Forex trading strategy: How to Invest with the Most Profitable and Simple Strategies to Make Money Trading Stocks, Options, Forex, Etfs in 2019 / 2020 Working Just 30 Minutes per Day.

Options Trading: The Best Beginner's Guide with All the Essential Information an Investor Needs on How the Options Market Works and How to Start Trading Options in 2019/2020.

www.ingramcontent.com/pod-product-compliance
Lightning Source LLC
Chambersburg PA
CBHW070337220526
45467CB00001B/150